Families of Emotionally Healthy College Students

William A. Westley
Nathan B. Epstein

the silent majority

Jossey-Bass Inc., Publishers
615 Montgomery Street • San Francisco • 1969

301.427
W 529

THE SILENT MAJORITY
Families of Emotionally Healthy College Students
by William A. Westley and Nathan B. Epstein

Library of Congress Catalog Card Number 77-75937

Standard Book Number SBN 87589-039-3

Manufactured in the United States of America
　　Composed and printed by York Composition Company, Inc.
　　Bound by Chas. H. Bohn & Co., Inc., New York
　　Jacket design by Willi Baum, San Francisco

FIRST EDITION

Code 6909

THE JOSSEY-BASS BEHAVIORAL SCIENCE SERIES

General Editors

WILLIAM E. HENRY, *University of Chicago*

NEVITT SANFORD, *Stanford University and Wright Institute, Berkeley*

Special Adviser in Adult Development

MARJORIE FISKE LOWENTHAL, *Langley-Porter Neuropsychiatric Institute, San Francisco*

Preface

The *Silent Majority* is a study of college students and their families. It is a deep sociopsychiatric probe into emotional health as manifested in the inner resources of these students and in the ways they handle their daily problems. Its aim is to determine how emotional health is related to the organization of these students' families.

There are striking differences in the organization of the families of emotionally healthy and emotionally disturbed students. Differences in the status of husband and wife at marriage, in the ways in which couples divide the housework and child care, in the pattern of authority within the family, and in the roles the parents play all affect the emotional health of the children and the kinds of personalities they develop. The roots of these differences lie in the relationship between the husband and wife. Couples who feel respect and affection for each other extend these feelings to their children, who grow up to become emotionally healthy persons.

These feelings in the family (respect and affection) are both reflected in and shaped by the organizational patterns the family adopts—to such an extent that these patterns are predictive of the emotional health of the children. How this discovery was made and how and why emotional health is linked to family life are the subject matter of this book.

The study was designed to profit from the depth and sensitivity of psychiatry and the scope and scientific rigor of sociology. Naturally, because of differences between the disciplines, many problems of synthesis and compromise arose. However, throughout the study, each discipline made its own contributions through independent though related work. What success the study may have achieved stems largely from the emphasis on this point, because the results were obtained by relating variations in social status and organization as defined and measured by the sociologist with variations in emotional health as defined and measured by the psychiatrist.

We have many debts. Not the least of them is to the students and their families who gave so freely of their time and shared their lives with us.

Many colleagues also contributed, directly or indirectly, to the study. We are especially indebted to Eric Wittkower and Frederick Elkin, who shared in the design of the pilot study and its field work and whose ideas enriched the work throughout. Nathan Wisebord, Pauline Lemyze, and Martha Lazure did all the psychological testing and screening, and Judith Simpson did most of the sociological interviewing and contributed to the data analysis in the comparative study. Alan Richardson and Cecile Kalifon-Solomon worked on data analysis. Helen Hughes was kind enough to revise the entire first draft.

The work could not, of course, have gone forward without considerable and patient financial support from various sources. The initial stages of the study were assisted by a Canadian Dominion Provincial Mental Health Grant. A calm summer of thoughtful discussion at the University of New Mexico was provided by the United States Air Force. The bulk of the funds was contributed in two major grants from the Foundations Fund for Research in Psychiatry.

Montreal   WILLIAM A. WESTLEY
March 1969   NATHAN B. EPSTEIN

Contents

the silent majority

CHAPTER 1

Ordinary Families

Our book reports the findings from two long-term, intensive, psychiatric-sociological studies designed to investigate the relationship between family organization and students' emotional health.

In the pilot study we explored the sources of emotional health in the families of college students shown by psychological tests and psychiatric interviews to possess exceptional emotional health. Both psychological and sociological aspects of the families' lives were studied. From these studies we derived hypotheses, which we then tested in a second study by comparing the families of emotionally healthy students with those of emotionally disturbed ones. The results of this comparative study confirmed our suspicion of an intimate relationship between the internal organization of the family and the emotional health of its members.

We tried to explain why the children in our families were

1

as emotionally healthy or disturbed as they were. Emotional health
was thus our major dependent variable. We measured it by getting
independent judgments from a psychiatrist who interviewed the
subjects and a psychologist who tested them with Rorschach and
Thematic Apperception (TAT) tests. Though the dimensions of
emotional health that they used clearly overlapped, the fact that
the two judges generally agreed on the exact degree of emotional
health in each subject indicates that the dimensions were not tautological.

We hypothesized that the differences in degree of emotional
health in the students were related to differences in the ways in
which their families were organized. The dimensions of family
organization that we used, such as status, division of labor, and
authority structure, were very clearly distinct from the criteria of
emotional health. For one thing, most of them rested on factors
that could not have been known or perceived by the judges—for
example, the relative social status of the husband and wife at the
time of marriage, or the division of labor in the family. Furthermore, although the psychiatrist, from his interviews, may have obtained clues to the power structure in the student's family, the
psychologist depended entirely on projective tests and could not
possibly have had such information. An additional insurance against
contamination was the fact that the questionnaire used to identify
and measure most of the organizational variables was devised and
administered only by the sociologist.

Thus our independent variable (family organization) was
clearly distinct from our dependent variable. In other words, what
we ultimately found to be some of the "causes" of emotional health
or illness in the students did not constitute part of the emotional
health judgments.

In its broadest terms, our problem was this: How does the
family affect the emotional development and health of its members?
Though it is now generally accepted that the family does play a
very influential role in the emotional health of children, little research has been done on the family itself. The traditional approach
to the family, which can be traced back to the pioneering work
of Freud, has emphasized the relationships between parents and

children, particularly mother and child, showing, especially, how deficiencies in mothering lead to emotional disturbance. The validity of these findings seems unquestionable. However, it should be recognized that such studies emphasize the mother-child relationship rather than family life.

Only very recently has the family itself become the focus of emotional health research. In psychiatry, the approach has been primarily through communications and transactional processes, for family psychiatrists are keenly aware of the emotional importance of these family interactions and have made significant therapeutic gains through changing them. While we, as researchers, maintain interest in and healthy respect for these studies, we are convinced that emotionally charged interactions are most influential when they become patterned in some more or less durable way. The pattern of interactions represents a constant of the family and constitutes a definite influence on the personalities of its members. In other words, it is our conviction that beneath the fluctuations of everyday family interaction there is a definite pattern, or organization, and that the fluctuations are contained by this pattern. Latitude for day-to-day variation is necessary if any organization is to meet the multitude of crises that constantly emerge from within itself and from its environment. However, adaptive processes must be controlled and limited. Control is accomplished by the organization that lends to these interactions the predictability necessary to understanding and cooperation and that orients them to the ends of the group. We believe that this organization is the most emotionally significant part of family life. This belief led to our search for dimensions of family organization and their relationship to the emotional health of family members.

The choice of the family as the unit of study can be justified not only by the results of psychoanalytic studies but also by sociological findings showing the strategic importance of the family in the health of its members. And in recent years sociologists have suggested that the nuclear family, composed of parents and children, is becoming of increasing emotional importance to its members. This group is probably the most durable and necessary of human social institutions. Though it is often embedded in more extensive kinship structures, it is always distinguished from the larger kin groups.

The concern with emotional health in this study reflects the staggering number of hospital beds that are now occupied by the emotionally ill and the discovery that a large proportion of the nonhospitalized population suffers from some fairly crippling emotional disorders. Traditionally, emotional health research has focused on patients, with the consequence that emotional health has been defined as the absence of illness. This definition is largely negative, stressing the absence rather than the presence of attributes. Since we disagree with this orientation, we have judged the degree of emotional health by the extent to which the person is using his mental and emotional resources, as well as by the absence of disorder symptoms. Furthermore, since we are primarily interested in the sources of emotional health, in contrast to illness, our research has been done on ordinary people who are functioning members of society, rather than on clinical cases.

The research took place in two phases. The first phase consisted of a pilot study of the families of ten emotionally healthy adolescents, the second, of a comparative study of the families of emotionally healthy and the families of emotionally disturbed adolescents. In all we studied 170 college students and eighty-eight families. The pilot study began in 1955 and took three years. The first year was devoted to screening the students, the second to the field study of their families, and the third to analysis and writing. On the basis of the results of this study we designed a larger study in which we could compare the families of emotionally healthy and the families of emotionally disturbed students. This larger study was started in 1958 and took six years. The first year was devoted to interviewing and testing the students, the next three years to field work with their families, and the last two years to analysis and writing. In 1964, nine years after the beginning of the pilot study, the final report was written.

The pilot study was based on the families of the ten most emotionally healthy among 170 college students. This group of 170 represented the entire population of first-year students who were from native-born, intact English Protestant families resident within ten miles of the university. The students were given the Gordon profile—a simple test of psychological adjustment—and the seventy best adjusted were also given Rorschach and TAT tests, as well as one-hour psychiatric interviews. Each student was independently rated as to his degree of emotional health by the psychiatrist and the psychologist. The ten students rated by both as the most healthy were then invited to participate, with their families, in a further intensive study.

The parents of these students were invited to a meeting with the research team at which the purpose and procedure of the study were explained and they were asked to cooperate in a further study of themselves. We explained that this would involve intensive and intimate study of the family over a long period of time. All these families agreed to cooperate. Subsequently, each member of each family was interviewed by the psychiatrist and also by the sociologist and given the Rorschach and TAT tests by the psychologist. Each parent was interviewed from ten to fifteen times for a total of from twenty to thirty hours. The interviews took place either in the home or research office, and in the case of the men, at least once in their occupational settings. Each child was also seen by each investigator, but more briefly. The interviews were semidirective, for we had a list of items covering personal life and family history that we brought up in each case, but since we were also interested in unique attributes we felt free to explore new areas when these seemed pertinent. Thus through this period there was a kind of unfolding as well as attrition of areas in which we were interested. Consequently, the data on subjects and families were not uniform, though it did turn out that we asked most of the same questions of each subject. When the field work was finished, we had intensive sociological, psychiatric, and psychological data on every member of these nine families. (Two of the students were twins.)

We then analyzed the data, identified the characteristics of families and life histories that we considered pertinent to family functioning or to the emotional health of family members, and developed crude hypotheses about the relationship between family organization and emotional health.

The intellectual problem was to identify the dimensions of family organization and of emotional health, then to find ways of measuring these dimensions so that variations in them might be compared from person to person and from family to family. We felt that we were able to identify and measure certain important dimensions, albeit in a very crude way, and that as a consequence we could make substantial gains in understanding this complicated area.

During the course of the pilot study we became convinced that the way in which a family organized itself and functioned as a unit was both a consequence and a cause of the mental health or illness of family members. It became clear to us that the married couple brought to their marriage their past (particularly the images of their own families) and their needs, which they had to work out within the limitations of the model of the family provided by their culture. Their success or failure in this task was, we felt, closely linked to their own subsequent emotional histories, and particularly to the emotional health of their children.

The selection process used in the comparative study differed from that of the pilot study only in that we were now equally interested in the students who were emotionally disturbed. We began by administering a simple socioeconomic questionnaire to the entire freshman English class, somewhat over 1,200 students. We were again looking for students from native-born, intact English Protestant families resident in Montreal. Of the 1,200 students who filled out the preliminary questionnaire, 104 fulfilled these qualifications. Subsequently, four of these were disqualified when we discovered that they did not in fact meet our socioeconomic criteria. The remainder were asked to cooperate in a psychiatric and psychological appraisal. For this purpose they were invited in groups of twenty to a series of meetings in which the purpose of the study was explained to them and they were asked for cooperation. At this point four more students dropped out, so only ninety-six actually completed the testing.

Each of these ninety-six students was interviewed for roughly an hour by the psychiatrist and given the TAT, the Rorschach, and a battery of pencil-and-paper and draw-a-picture tests by the psychologist. On the basis of the information that each had gathered, the psychiatrist and the psychologist made independent ratings of the emotional health of each student. A rank-order correlation of .75 between their ratings, which was significant at better than the .01 level of probability, showed a high degree of agreement. Actually, most of their ratings were identical or in adjoining categories. Where they did not agree, we averaged their ratings, except where these ratings were in adjoining categories, in which case we accepted the rating of the psychiatrist. All cases of disagreement were discussed in conference, and in a few cases both raters readjusted their ratings.

On the basis of these ratings the students were divided into three groups, consisting of the twenty healthiest, the twenty most disturbed, and those in between. The parents of each group were then invited to a meeting in which the research team explained the purpose and procedures of the study and asked their cooperation. They were told in great detail exactly what would be asked of them, and they were promised nothing except absolute anonymity and an opportunity to contribute to an important area of scientific knowledge. They were told nothing about the emotional health ratings of their children. In fact we told them that all the ratings and interviews would be absolutely confidential, so that the parents would be refused the information that their children had given us. We also told them that we would not provide any therapeutic assistance, though we would refer them to appropriate persons and agencies if they so requested.

The proportion of each group who agreed to cooperate in the study constituted a surprising confirmation of our emotional health ratings. When the families are divided into four groups, arranged in order from the families of the healthiest students to those of the most disturbed, we found that 90 per cent of the ten families in group one, 79 per cent of the thirty-one families in group two, 52 per cent of the forty-one families in group three, and only 20 per cent of the ten families in group four agreed to cooperate in the study. This was our first intimation of the difference between the ways in which the families of healthy and of disturbed subjects met crises. The healthy seemed to welcome new experience as a way of enriching and deepening life; the disturbed only felt threatened and attempted to withdraw. The proportions also gave us our first information about the differences between people who do and those who do not cooperate in research.

With the agreement of the families to cooperate in the research, we were able to begin the field work. Since the heart of this study was the comparison of the families of emotionally healthy and the families of emotionally disturbed adolescents, we divided the families into three groups: those of the ten healthiest subjects, those of the ten most disturbed subjects, and those of the subjects who fell in between. We had decided to concentrate our attention on the two extreme groups and limit the time we gave to the larger group in between. Consequently, all members of the families in the extreme groups were interviewed by both the sociologist and the psychiatrist, and also given the TAT and Rorschach tests by the psychologist and a seventy-page sociological questionnaire by a sociological research assistant. The members of the families in the middle group were seen only by the psychologist, who gave each of them the TAT and Rorschach tests, and by the sociological research assistant, who administered the sociological questionnaire. Thus our data for the families in the extreme groups were both more extensive and reliable than those for the families in the middle group, since we had the additional information supplied by the sociological and psychiatric interviews as well as a "second opinion" on their emotional health.

Ordinarily, the field work was initiated by arranging an informal evening in which the sociologist and psychiatrist could get acquainted with the whole family. We used this visit to get the cooperation of the members of the family whom we had not seen before, particularly the younger children. In doing this, we went to some lengths to explain the study and encouraged the family members to ask questions about the project and about us, and to express any doubts or uneasiness they felt. We found the families of the emotionally healthy subjects to be very lively and often somewhat anxious. They usually expressed this anxiety and asked for clarification. The families of the disturbed subjects often tended to be rigidly casual, pretending complete informality and cooperation, while actually being very hostile and withdrawn. During the course of the preliminary visit we arranged interviews with the individual members of the family as a way of making their cooperation secure. Our interviews were followed by those of the psychologist and the sociological assistant.

Our data, then, consisted of the following: For each member of the families of the ten healthiest and the ten most disturbed subjects we had from one to three psychiatric interviews, one sociological interview, a seventy-page questionnaire covering all aspects of personal and family life, TAT protocols, a psychiatric evaluation, and a psychological evaluation. All interviews and TAT protocols were dictated on tape the same day in an effort to retain as much as possible of the original wording. In addition, for each of the original subjects we had a battery of thirty-eight pencil-and-paper tests drawn from the Minnesota Multiphasic Personality Inventory (MMPI), the Vassar Personality Scale, the California Psychological Inventory, and the Guilford-Zimmerman Inventory.

There was, of course, varied cooperation from the families, but as in the response to the first request for cooperation, the families of the healthiest subjects were completely cooperative, always meeting their interview appointments and seldom complaining about the questions, while those of the most disturbed subjects often canceled interviews, sometimes tried to withdraw or actually did withdraw from the study, and frequently complained about the questions, particularly those of a very personal nature. Yet even the people from these families, who obviously found the study very threatening, often tried very hard to cooperate and would insist on continuing with interviews despite the fact that they sometimes cried all through them. Of course, we did not insist that anyone continue with the project or give us information in any particular area. But we always found that if the family was prepared to go through with the interviews they would give us whatever information we asked for, provided we took care to explain why we needed it and reaffirmed their complete anonymity, explaining that most of the material would be presented in statistical form.

It was interesting to note that among the cooperating families those in the middle group proved to be the most recalcitrant.

In some cases a member of the family, usually the father, refused to make appointments, and canceled those he had made, until we were forced to get the information we required from another member of the family. We assume that the difference in the degree of cooperation of this group of families was due to the difference in the prestige of the investigators and to the fact that we did not make the informal preliminary visits. As a consequence, some of these families dropped out, and in the case of others we concluded the field work without psychological reports or sociological questionnaires from some of the members.

We studied the entire universe of families who met our criteria of selection—that is, the families of first-year McGill University students who were native-born, of English Protestant stock, intact, and resident in Montreal. The criteria of intactness and ethnic homogeneity were designed to eliminate the influence of variables like culture and degree of family organization. First-year college students were chosen because this is the youngest age group on which we felt that a reasonably reliable psychiatric assessment could be made. Other criteria of selection, such as the particular university and residence in Montreal, were adopted for reasons of practicality.

The sample is probably representative of families from this ethnic group who send children to the university. One can, of course, ask whether differences in family organization are likely to have the effects they did only in this group, but we have no reason to believe that such a limitation would prevail. It should be noted, however, that our sample showed a slight bias toward emotional health, with 26 per cent well, 30 per cent showing mild symptoms, 30 per cent showing moderate symptoms, and 14 per cent showing definite impairment. In contrast, the Sterling County Study (Leighton et al., 1963) showed 17 per cent of its population well and 20 per cent definitely impaired, and the Midtown Manhattan Study (Srole et al., 1962), 18.5 per cent well and 23.4 per cent definitely impaired. Given the errors arising from our attempt to establish comparative categories and the lower age and higher socioeconomic status of our sample, the slight bias toward emotional health in our study is understandable.

A potential source of bias arose when many families refused to cooperate. Only fifty-nine of the ninety-seven families chosen agreed to be studied. Furthermore, the thirty-eight families who refused to participate were primarily those of the more emotionally disturbed students. This concerned us in two ways. First, we wanted to know if through these refusals we had lost comparative groups of families of emotionally disturbed adolescents. A check revealed that this was not the case, since we found that the families of the disturbed who agreed to be studied did contain seriously disturbed children and that the fifty-nine cooperating families were distributed in a smooth continuum from health to disturbance. Second, we wanted to know whether the families who refused to cooperate were different from those who agreed, in terms of our major organizational variables. Fortunately, we had a check on this since twenty of the students from these families were persuaded to contribute detailed information about their families. When these families were compared with disturbed families who had cooperated, we could find no consistent differences. In other words, with respect to our major independent variables, families who refused were similar to those who cooperated—to such an extent, in fact, that we confidently added them to the sample in analyzing those variables on which they had provided solid information. Yet we recognize that there must have been some characteristic that differentiated the refusing families from the others, and it remains a puzzle and a source of concern.

Finally, we should point out that to some extent the size of the sample varied with the variable under analysis, because in some areas we were not able to get the same information from all the families. For example, detailed information about sex relations was obtained only from the families in the pilot study and from the ten most healthy and ten most disturbed families in the major study. In other cases where the variable was scored on the basis of responses to the questionnaire, we found that many families had either failed or refused to answer so many of the pertinent questions that their scores were not reliable. In these cases we felt it much better to include only those families whose responses were reliable.

Certainly, these deficiencies in the sample reduce its effectiveness. We recognized this, but we also recognized that for the kind of study we were making—that is, an intensive psychiatric-sociological study of families—our sample was probably more representative, and in most ways more satisfactory, than those of most other intensive psychiatric family studies, which have been confined to very small samples exclusively from the clinical population. Furthermore, we reasoned that insofar as we had reasonable variation in our major dependent and independent variables, we could establish whether in fact they were related.

THE FAMILIES

The families in our study lived in Montreal, whose population of over a million people makes it the largest city in Canada and the second largest French-speaking city in the world. Thus it is a bilingual city, within which the English have historically been a minority, though economically dominant. Besides the French Catholics, who constitute more than 65 per cent of the population, and the English Protestants, who form another 18 per cent, there are various other national and religious groups, of which the most numerous are the Italians, the Eastern European Jews, the Germans, and the Poles, in that order.

Though the families who joined the study stemmed originally from all over Canada, 65 per cent of their members had been born and brought up in Montreal. Most of the others had migrated from adjoining provinces, a movement whose effect was to separate them from their relatives and to convert them into the isolated nuclear units typical of modern industrial society. These families had almost nothing to do with their relatives. This was not, of course, true of those who had been born and brought up in Montreal, many of whom saw siblings of the husband and wife as frequently as once a week or oftener. We did not, however, get the impression that they were in any way a part of an extended family or clan.

Most of the participants seemed to be typical urbanites, lacking in friends, distant from their neighbors, and attached to the community only through their work and, in some cases, their churches and service clubs. The parents visited other couples about every two weeks. About one-third attended club meetings at least once a month, and one-third reported that they often went to church. Most seemed to feel little identification with the community. It is true that when their children were younger they were all more closely involved with their residential community, but those ties seem to have withered as the children matured. Thus, except for some families that kept in close contact with relatives, the attachments of these people to the city were formal and tenuous. These were metropolitan people, used to living in a community too large and complex to know or really be part of. They lived in it, but it was not part of them.

Most of the families were of the middle, upper-middle, or upper class, as judged by Hollingshead's (Hollingshead and Redlich, 1958) index based on education, occupation, and place of residence. Sixty-four of the seventy-nine families were drawn from the middle and upper-middle classes.*

Typically, the Class II (upper-middle-class) family lived in an owner-occupied house in one of the newer areas of the city. The husband-father had a university education and was an executive in a large firm, with an annual salary of approximately $15,000. The family had enough money for travel and for the education of their children and enough, too, for pleasure and entertainment. In these families the wife-mother usually had a college education also. She did most of her own housework, with the help of a weekly cleaning woman, and still managed time for leisure and recreation in the afternoons.

In contrast, the Class III (middle-class) family lived in a smaller home and generally in an older middle-class area or one of new, modestly priced areas. The father had finished high school, and in many cases college, and was a lower-level executive, typically in the sales department. His annual income was about $10,-000, so, especially with a child in college, the family had to keep a tight rein on expenses. Ordinarily, the funds available for travel or entertainment were limited. The mother, also high school educated, did all her own housework.

* Class was not computed for the nine families in the pilot study.

The contrast between these two groups of families and those from the upper and lower classes was marked. The upper-class families, with incomes of at least $25,000, had surplus funds, a great deal of household help, and considerable leisure; the lower-class families, on the other hand, were beset by economic problems, which amplified the amount of necessary work, so that leisure seemed out of the question.

Since the father's job is probably the family's most important connection with the community, it is important to describe the family in terms of it. Table 1 shows the distribution of the father's occupations in this study.

Table 1

OCCUPATIONS OF FATHERS

Category	Frequency
Unskilled worker	1
Semiskilled worker	0
Skilled worker	2
Owner of small business, clerical or sales worker, or technician	10
Administrator in large concern or semiprofessional	24
Manager or owner of medium-sized company or lesser professional	30
Major professional, executive, or manager of large business	12

Most of the husbands and wives in our sample had at least high school educations. Although wives tended to have somewhat less education than husbands, the level of the husband's education provides a reasonable indication of the wife's. Ten fathers did not finish high school, twenty-seven finished high school, twenty-nine went to college, and eleven had graduate or professional training.

In most cases our families had experienced considerable social mobility. Most of the grandfathers were middle class or lower, in contrast to most of the fathers, who were middle class or higher. Many of the grandfathers had been tradesmen or small farmers without much education, and a large part of them had emigrated from the United Kingdom. Most of the fathers in our sample had improved their status by attaining more education, better jobs, and higher incomes than their own fathers. However, they had grown up in a period characterized by a general upward trend in education and income, and their successes cannot be regarded entirely as unique personal achievements.

All of the seventy-nine families were intact, with both parents alive and with no divorces or remarriages at the time of the study. The families were small, over 70 per cent having either two or three children. The distribution was as follows: Thirteen families had one child; twenty-nine families, two children; twenty-six families, three children; ten families, four children; and one family, five children. The mean family size was 2.5 children. The families of orientation of the parents were often considerably larger; over 25 per cent of the families of the fathers and 8 per cent of the families of the mothers had six or more children. Approximately 15 per cent of the households in our sample contained an aged grandparent.

Daily routines in many ways communicate more about the living fabric of the family than the bare bones of our statistics. The daily lives of these families seemed remarkably similar. In general, the day began at 7 A.M. with the mother rising to prepare breakfast and the rest of the family eating and leaving for school or work. In some families the fathers got up first to prepare the coffee or breakfast. In others that were less affluent the wife got up at about 5 A.M. to do the housework, prepare breakfast, and pack lunches for herself and her family before she herself left for work.

Then, with the men off to work and the children off to school, all the women who did not work turned to housework, ordinarily devoting a particular day to heavy housecleaning or laundry. Most of the women finished this work by noon, so that, unless they had younger children or husbands coming home for lunch, they were free for the afternoon. Most of them tried to preserve this period as a time for themselves. Many went out of the house to meet friends, go shopping, or pursue an interest; others read or took naps.

The house again made demands on them between 4 and 5 P.M., when the children were usually home and it was time to prepare dinner. Many women made a point of keeping the time just before dinner for their husbands, with whom they might have a drink and talk over the day's events. This was a time when families began to show considerable variation, for some men did not come home until very late and others did not talk with their wives at this time. However, in most families it was a time of social contact, and the nature of the contact or its avoidance reflected the emotional relationships. It was also a time when many members of the family were tired, so that irritations and hostilities came to the surface easily.

With dinner over, another set of routines was put into motion. Frequently the other members of the family, particularly the daughters, helped the mother with the cleaning up, and then the children turned to homework and the parents to reading or television. This was also a time of activities for the parents—for going out, visiting friends, and participating in community service, sports, music, or other interests.

In making a detailed study of the activities in which these families engaged, we found that some were extremely active, while others did practically nothing. However, it was quite clear that for most the evenings were used principally for relaxation, watching television, reading newspapers or books, and listening to the radio or to music. Most of the parents went out or had friends in at least once a week, though again there was considerable variation, some families doing twice as much entertaining and others almost none at all. In fact, we were surprised to find that some of these urban families seemed to lead almost completely isolated lives, with absolutely no friends and no outside activities; yet they remained quite contented and felt they had rich and full lives. In certain areas, such as politics and clubs, a few families were extremely active, many others inactive. Yet the picture emerged of a group of families who spent most of their free time in quiet spectator activities. In many cases these activities were the main basis of family interaction.

During the weekends the household routines became more loosely structured. Some families went away to cottages and some visited relatives, but most stayed at home. Many husbands did a bit more to help their wives; some men brought their work home. Some women used the weekend for intensive housecleaning, often with the help of their daughters. But in general weekends were viewed as a time for family life, relaxation, and pleasure.

In summary, our families were mostly middle-class, well-educated, moderately prosperous people who seemed to be responsible, relatively settled in their ways, and moderate in their views. They were ordinary people, not too deeply involved in politics or religion, but friendly and willing, and relatively happy in their lives. Most of the parents were devoted to each other and their children, and friendly with their relatives when they met. On these points the interviewers agreed. All these people were functioning as successful and responsible members of the community and regarded as well adapted to their way of life. All the men held jobs, and some could be described as leading industrialists. Most of the women were housewives. The average family income was high, and each family had at least one child in the university. The general physical health of the family members was good and none was insane. These were families that had never been and probably would never become problems to the social agencies or appear in mental hospitals. They were, in moral terms, good, honest people, living conventional lives, struggling to meet their problems, and giving no trouble to anyone. Ordinarily, we know little about such people precisely because they present few problems and mind their own business.

These, then, were the people who agreed to help us find out how families function and whether their functioning bears any relationship to the personalities or mental health of their members. We were able to obtain from them detailed and intimate information about all aspects of their lives and their emotional reactions to fundamental and mundane problems. They let us probe deeply into their experiences, thoughts, and reactions, many of which had been completely private until then.

As our inquiry proceeded, we began to see differences among the families, and our interest magnified these differences until they loomed large. Clearly the families were far from "perfect": they all had problems of one kind or another, whether marital, economic, or child-related. Though in most cases they were attractive and admirable people, they often suffered from some personal deficiency: in the capacity to express tenderness, rage, or sexuality, or to assert themselves or deal with depression; in sexual or other kinds of identity; or in the ability to make friends or relate to other people. Most, however, found ways of coping with their particular problems.

We were astonished at some of the adaptations they had made. Some of the parents had almost no sex life but were affectionate, happy, well adjusted and blessed with emotionally healthy, competent children. Others, who seemed to be afflicted with every other kind of difficulty, including poor sexual identification, enjoyed a full sex life. However, there were families who were enormously successful and powerful but unbelievably crippled in their family life, emotionally isolated from each other and themselves, propped up only by their wealth. In some cases we were struck by the toughness and resilience we saw, in others by the incredible fragility.

On our first meeting with each family we spent a sociable evening with them just to get acquainted and to gain their confidence. At the conclusion of each such meeting we would exchange impressions. Sometimes we found that we had been badly mistaken: A family that at first sight seemed tense and ill adapted to life later turned out to be remarkably well adjusted; another, apparently happy and socially competent, was, in fact, sorely tried and often coping poorly. Fortunately for our self-confidence, our first impressions were not usually so wrong, but they were wrong often enough to make us realize how skilled some families could become in creating an acceptable façade.

As we talked to the family members individually, we came

to respect more and more their honesty and courage in participating in our study. They all endured considerable strain from time to time, and some even reached the point of tears. Naturally, we did not expect that they would always be able or willing to tell us the truth, for discrimination in recall and the strong emotional loading of the subjects about which we were inquiring were bound to bring about some distortion. But it was clear they were trying their best to cooperate, and various checks, such as internal consistency or the corroboration of a story by various family members, indicated that they told us the truth.

THE STUDENTS

Our original subjects were university freshmen ranging in age from seventeen through twenty, the mean age being eighteen and a half years. Two-thirds of them were boys. When we first met them, they were barely out of high school and therefore young in ideas and experience as well as years. Since they were almost all still living at home, there was a distinct continuity between home and university life. Their families continued to be a daily source of security and control. Thus in most cases these young people had neither achieved independence nor met the strains and maturation it entails. This was particularly true of heterosexual relations, about which even the healthiest and boldest boys expressed timidity.

Very few of these students had had any sexual experience and some were so thoroughly frightened by sex that they had avoided even the mildest forms of petting. Some had never even had a date. The norm was conservative. But most of the students were deeply concerned with and excited by the problems of heterosexuality. They looked forward to sexual relations, but felt uneasy. A surprising number of boys said that they intended to remain chaste until after marriage—an attitude, incidentally, in which they weakened remarkably in the succeeding few years.

Most of the students were testing family bonds and exploring the idea of independence, but, except for a few, there was no rebellion. They were developing the yen to be on their own, but they were not yet ready to do anything about it, except for a summer's work away from home. When the study began they were still very much part of their families, attached to and dependent on their parents. And since 70 per cent were either first or only children, most of the families were still functioning as complete units. Seventy per cent were first or only children, 10 per cent were middle children, and 19 per cent were last born. The fact that 70 per cent of our subjects were either first-born or only children probably means that there is some bias in our findings, since these children experienced their parents' first experimental attempts at child-rearing, were the most likely objects of role projections, and always found themselves playing the role of the eldest. However, we found no relationship between birth order and the emotional health of the children.

The students' experiences in high school covered the spectrum from high sociability in clubs and dating to relative isolation. We noted that high frequency seemed to be related to emotional health and low frequency to emotional disturbance, but we found no such association with dating. We had information on dating from only fifty subjects. The median age for the beginning of dating was about fourteen years, but most of the subjects did very little dating at this age, or, for that matter, while they were in high school. Except during the last years, dating was largely a matter of a few dances and parties, although there were a few couples who saw a great deal of each other. Among the twenty-nine students who reported that they had dated less than once a week while they were in high school, there were a considerable number who had not dated at all at that time, and there were some who still had not had a date when they were first interviewed as first-year college students.

We also asked the students about church attendance and found that 50 per cent never went to church, except possibly once a year on a major holiday, and that only 25 per cent went to church as much as three times a month. Nor did we find that religion played much part in their daily or family lives. Only a few prayed regularly or said grace at meals. Many of them were interested in discussing religion, but this probably reflected the perennial freshman and sophomore bull-session orientation to such topics, plus the ebullient interest, typical of their age, in "the meaning of life."

Most of our subjects were good students. We made a search for their grades in the various schools within the university, and though we were not successful in finding all the records of all our students, we did find enough to give us a clear picture of their academic work. Roughly half of these students had an average grade of 65 or better, which gave them a second-class standing at McGill. Three students failed in the first year, fourteen in the second, and three in the third.

These students did not, in our estimation, fit the current stereotypes of college students in North America, though we suspect that they may well be quite representative. Most of them were serious about, without being dedicated to, their studies, and, as might be expected of middle-class students, showed marks better than the average. Some had begun the process of constructing their own lives in high school, where they were active in school life, began dating, took jobs, and had a wide circle of friends. But a great many were still deeply attached to their families and showed few real signs of independence.

These were the people who agreed to enter the study and who, for extensive periods of time, shared their lives with us. Their cooperation enabled us to utilize the method we had devised to measure the many facets and dimensions of family life. Our analysis of the data was a long and painstaking process during which many treasured hypotheses were discarded. But it was also a time of great excitement and discovery, as some leading ideas were confirmed and unexpected relationships discovered. The bulk of this book describes our findings. It confirms, in our estimation, the tremendous importance of organization to the viability of the family and the emotional health of its members.

CHAPTER **2**

Family Patterns

Organization, or the durable modes of relationship between the members of the family, is described in terms of five dimensions: power, psychodynamics, roles, status, and work. We assume that variations in each dimension can be measured or categorized and that by describing the family in terms of these dimensions we describe its organization. Function refers to the consequences of particular kinds of family organization for the psychological, social, and cultural needs of its members. Here we assume that all people have needs on each of these levels, and we postulate that different kinds of organization differ in the degree to which they can meet these needs.

Theories of needs are generally accepted by psychiatrists, tolerated by many psychologists, and regarded with suspicion by sociologists. The suspicion is grounded in the difficulty of constructing valid operational definitions. Because of this difficulty lists of needs range from the four wishes of Thomas (1924) to much more elaborate systems, such as those of Murray (1938), and it is very difficult to support one instead of another. Yet it is also difficult to escape the idea that some concept of needs is essential to the explanation of much human behavior. Any voluntaristic-learning theory of personality must include the idea that men have predispositions, wants, or needs, which, while not determinant, definitely influence their conduct.

It is important, however, to keep in mind the derivation of the idea of needs. Obviously, to say that men act because of needs is a way of saying that they will act in certain ways in certain circumstances. Thus to say that they have a need for affection is merely a way of describing that they do indeed seek and appreciate affection and become frustrated if they do not obtain it.

The reasons why they act in these ways are manifold. We know from interviews and from introspection that men share the goals and values of their societies, so that they literally want what society values. We also accept certain crude physical needs like hunger, thirst, and, less unequivocally, the need for sexual gratification. At the same time, we know that the ways in which these needs are met do not seem to be determined by the body, except within wide limits.

We have chosen to divide man's needs into three categories: psychological, social, and cultural. Needs are psychological when they are derived from the structure of the personality, social when they arise as part of the interaction process, and cultural when they appear as internalized values or expectations of the community.

Certain psychological needs, which can be identified though not operationally defined, seem to be common to all men. Others, peculiar to particular individuals, are shaped out of general needs by early interpersonal experiences. For our purpose, the reader need accept only the idea that the members of a family inevitably make various psychological demands on each other. The influence of psychological needs on marriage is recognized and reflected in descriptions of husband-wife relationships in terms of complementary needs—for example, as dominance-submission or sado-masochism. The bride and groom bring to their relationship both the psychological needs that they possess as human beings and those that they have acquired from their previous life experiences. If their needs are reciprocal and nondestructive, such that each can meet the demands of the other without punishment, they will tend to arrange their relationships to meet those needs. Social needs arise within the family itself. Husband, wife, and children, as members of a group, need to interact and cooperate, and can be either frustrated or satisfied in these needs. Thus the family must be sufficiently organized to permit it to function and to meet the everyday needs of its members. If the system of communication is deficient, it is difficult to cooperate and reach common ends, to express and claim satisfaction for personal needs, and to adjust differences. If the system of authority is deficient, decision making is imperiled and conflict threatens. Without adequate division of labor, the work of the family never gets done. Inadequacies in any of these organizational dimensions ramify into the more sensitive and complex interpersonal life of the family members. Since social needs arise because the family is a social group, in which the daily tasks must be completed, decisions made, and conflicts resolved, the well-being and even the survival of the family members may depend on an at least minimal degree of success in all these things.

The family's fate is intertwined with that of the community, since the family has social, economic, and political involvements with and responsibilities toward the community. Therefore the members of the family tend to evaluate themselves and each other in terms of the values and anticipated reactions of the community. Effectively, then, cultural needs consist of demands made on the self and others as a result of the internalization of community values. These values affect the organization of the family since they function to legitimize certain forms of organization, and thus also affect the members of the family, since the experience of acting legitimately enhances the ego.

The dimensions of organization that we studied (power, psychodynamics, roles, status, and work)* can be seen as responses

* Levy (1949) has called these dimensions: role differentiation, allocation of solidarity, economic allocation, political allocation, and the allocation of integration and expression.

to generic problems faced by all families. They resemble the functional prerequisites of social systems formulated by Parsons (1951). Except for status, each has already been the subject of considerable family research: Roles, power, and division of labor are familiar to family sociologists and social psychologists, and psychodynamic organization to psychiatrists. However, to our knowledge these dimensions have never been seen as a cluster, nor has there been an attempt to specify criteria for evaluating the consequences of variations in them. We have chosen five dimensions that we consider important. The list is not exhaustive, since it omits others, like the system of communications, that we could not accurately measure or categorize.

The best studied of our five dimensions of family organization is power, which is recognized as a critical aspect of all organizations and is often linked in family life to the drives and personalities of the children. It is alleged to have a goal-direction function, in the sense that it is the chief means by which the group coordinates its activities toward its goals. In studies of the family it is most often defined in terms of decision making, though sometimes in terms of dominance and conflict resolution. Zelditch (1964) has pointed out that the diverse ways in which balance of power has been operationally defined make comparison between studies difficult. Yet despite the diversity of studies and definitions, there is considerable consistency in findings showing that families do vary in the ways in which they distribute power and that these variations are related to social class and ethnicity (Zedlich, 1964), the relative competence of husband and wife (Blood and Wolfe, 1960), achievement motivation in children (Strodtbeck, 1958), and psychopathology (Clausen and Kohn, 1960; King and Henry, 1955). Many studies, however, either isolate the balance of power from other dimensions of family organization (Herbst, 1952) or fail to differentiate it from some of them (Zedlich, 1964), thus weakening findings about the causes or effects of variations in the balance of power.

Few studies provide theories that can explain such causes or effects. We suggest an analysis in terms of needs of the family members: (1) The psychological needs of husband and wife definitely influence and are affected by the balance of power, and spouses probably tend to shape the power relationship in terms of them. Yet a conflict of needs within or between the marital partners will make any power arrangement unsatisfactory. Thus if the wife rules it may satisfy their inclinations to dominance-submission, but it will probably frustrate some of their sexual needs. (2) It is difficult to distinguish between what we have called social needs and the balance of power in the family, though it seems clear that the "need" of the family for decisions and conflict resolution requires some agreement about the relative authority and responsibility of the husband and wife. Yet the particular balance of power seems to be affected by the relative competence of the husband and wife (Blood and Wolfe, 1960). (3) Cultural needs appear as preferences for or uneasiness about a particular balance of power. Since the legitimization of power within the family is derived from the culture (Komarovsky, 1940), it seems reasonable that the approved conventional forms will be preferred and deviations avoided.*

Our measures of the balance of power were based on scores given to the relative influence of husband and wife in discipline, decision making, and conflict resolution, as well as on estimations by each member of the family of the relative dominance of each of the parents and the way in which the family makes decisions. Questions relating to each of these areas were scored for both the husband and the wife (if they shared a responsibility, both received scores for that item). The proportion of the combined scores achieved by each was then computed. From the results we distinguished five types of authority: *father-dominant* (the father received more than 65 per cent), *father-led* (the father received 56–65 per cent), *equalitarian* (the father received 45–55 per cent), *mother-led* (the mother received 56–65 per cent), and *mother-dominant* (the mother received more than 65 per cent).

The psychodynamic organization of the family refers to the emotional relationships between its members, as seen and ordered by psychoanalytic concepts. It includes the variety of emotional roles played by members and imposed on each other. The family

* To our knowledge Komarovsky is the only student of family life who has recognized the importance of legitimization.

can be seen as a set of such relationships between husband and wife, parent and child, and child and child. Each relationship differs from the others, reflecting differences in role, sex, power, and education, as well as the particular meanings that family members have for one another. The bases of such relationships are complex, and their quality reflects these complexities. Particularly significant is the fact that the relationship between father and mother affects and is affected by the relationship between each of them and the children.

Our studies identified two general variables involved in psychodynamic organization: problem solution and autonomy. Each is a summary term for complex patterns of organization, rather than a clear single dimension.

Problem solution refers to the ability of a family to recognize and deal with emotional problems in or between its members. It is reflected in the pattern of interaction, rapport, and sympathy among the members. The number and severity of the problems that families face vary considerably, depending on personalities and life stresses. But every family inevitably gives rise to some problems in the management of emotions. Its ability to recognize and resolve, rather than avoid or deny, these problems is crucial to its life as a family. Obviously, problems that are recognized and dealt with tend to disappear, while those that are not may accumulate and aggravate each other.

Autonomy refers to the degree to which members of a family respect, permit, and encourage private and independent emotional lives in the others. It is particularly manifest and critical for the children, whose growth should, and usually does, include increased independence. Some families encourage the development of autonomy, but others can or will not. Parents may need the dependency of their children or each other, and may resist tendencies toward independence. At the same time, children are fond of the safety of their dependency and somewhat fearful of autonomy.

The family requires work, both for income and for the care of its members. The functioning of a household requires cooking, mending, cleaning, repairs, shopping, and attention to a thousand and one details. Labor is a necessity imposed on the family. And how its members meet it has important consequences for the system of interpersonal relationships. As Homans (1950) has noted, the system of work guides interaction, which, in turn, governs senti-ment. But what shapes the form of the system of work? We think the most important force is precedent. The family backgrounds of husband and wife are the models by which they construct their own family. Tradition and cultural expectations regarding the proper role of husband and wife are inherent in this force. The socioeconomic setting—that is, the community, social mobility, class level, and husband's occupation—also affects the system of work. For example, a man who works from 7 A.M. to 7 P.M. usually does little around the house. Spouses in mobile families, since they are cut off from kin, have a greater need for sharing and conse-quently a more even division of labor.*

The psychological needs of the husband and wife provide the third force in determining the allotment of work. A soft male with a great need to take care of others may participate heavily in mothering and its attendant tasks, like shopping and cooking, while a hard, strong-willed woman who fears her own sexuality may take over many traditionally male tasks, such as control of finance and a share in earning the living.

Though it is theoretically possible that one person could both support the family and do all the housework, this usually hap-pens only when one parent is incapacitated or absent. Ordinarily, the work is divided, with the man providing the support and the woman doing the housework and taking care of the children. It seems rare, certainly in North America, for the woman to be solely responsible for the housework and child care, and one finds various degrees of sharing. These can be described along a continuum of male participation in housework and child care, the male doing, at one extreme, almost none of these things, at the other, most of them.

We described the division of labor in the family by allocat-ing scores to the husband and wife and to both of them together

---

* Bott (1957) has shown that the division of labor also reflects the psychological climate of the family, which is interwoven with its socioeco-nomic setting.

on the basis of a modified version of the Herbst task questionnaire (thirty-eight household tasks) in which we asked each member of the family whether first the father and then the mother did each task often, sometimes, or never. From the total scores we computed what proportion of the responsibilities were taken by the husband alone, the wife alone, and both together. Using these proportions, we identified four types of division of labor: *traditional,* where the husband-father shares almost none of the household tasks and has few, or none, as his sole responsibility; *balanced,* where he takes responsibility for roughly a seventh of the tasks and shares another fifth with his wife; *sharing,* where the husband and wife share more tasks than either does alone; and *unconventional,* where the husband takes responsibility for more tasks than does his wife. We discovered that these differences in types of division of labor are related to differences in family functioning and emotional health.

The family is a field in which the members play out their status in the larger society, so that these external positions come to affect the relationships between the members of the family. Thus external status becomes internal status.

The status—primarily the occupation—of the father is usually the key to status interaction in the family. His psychological response to his status experience may be played out in the family in the ways he socializes his children, treats his wife, and plays his family roles. His external status also affects how he appears to the other members, so it is an important determinant of his status within the family. It has consequences for the others, for it determines their social status and life chances and influences their self-images. How it affects them depends to some extent on their own status careers. The wife who has lost status because of her marriage reacts differently from the one who has gained. Similarly, the boy who has been successful in school or peer group is less dependent for self-esteem on the status of the father.

We used the status and mobility experiences of the father and the mother during the course of their marriage as an indicator of status relationships within the family. Basing measure of status experience on Hollingshead's (1958) two-factor index (education and occupation), we computed the status scores of the husband

and wife as well as those of their fathers, and from them we computed mobility. For example, the intergenerational mobility of the wife was computed by subtracting the status score of her husband from that of her father. The difference indicates whether she was mobile, as well as the extent and direction of her mobility. Since she is dependent on her husband for this mobility, it seemed probable that her mobility would affect their relationship—that is, that she would praise or blame him in the myriad subtleties of conjugal life. Our data show that her mobility is related both to their sexual appreciation of each other and to the personalities of their children.

Ultimately, the functioning of the family is dependent on its institutionalization: Only as the emotional relationships, division of labor, and authority of the family are structured by norms will they function in a dependable fashion, or in such a way that the needs of the members, the family itself, and the larger community are met in a relatively routine fashion. In a successful family these routine norms will be mutually supportive. A man's role, for example, is composed of his sex, his occupation, and his parenthood. As Parsons (1951) has noted, success in one area (for example, work) may be necessary to success in another (sex). On the other hand, failures or contradictions impose strains on the family. For example, the upwardly mobile male may find little congruence between the occupational and marital definitions of his role.

The modern family suffers from the lack of such institutionalization, for while the old definitions have weakened with the paring away of old functions, the new definitions and norms have not become clear or firmly fixed. This lack of fixed norms gives an undue amount of influence to psychodynamic needs, leading to much conflict and disorganization in the family.

We measured roles in terms of the degree to which the husband and wife accepted and participated in their roles of worker, spouse, and parent, and then analyzed interviewer protocols to judge role acceptance. Drawing upon the questionnaires, we then learned the spouses' reports on the extent to which they did certain kinds of work and participated in particular kinds of activities. Our findings show a relationship between spouse and parent roles and the emotional health of the children.

An organization is adequate when it meets its members' needs. We used psychiatric and psychological judgments of emotional health to estimate how well the family met psychological needs, the efficiency of the family in work and decision making as criteria of its adequacy in meeting social needs, and social status as a reflection of its adequacy in meeting cultural needs. Using these criteria, we compared the functional efficiency of variations in each organizational element. In each case we found that the pattern of organization that most successfully met the members' psychological, social, and cultural needs identified the families who seemed most durable and adaptable, with the emotionally healthiest members.

Of course, the type of organization that is optimal depends on the family's composition and socioeconomic status. Large, extended, poor Mexican-American families obviously face different problems from small, aristocratic New England families, and the form of organization suitable to one may be useless to the other.

The division of labor in the family is a source of identity and gratification for the members, inasmuch as it is a means of differentiating sex roles and sustaining the psychology of sexual attractiveness. It can also be a source of confusion and conflict. It can be the instrument by which the members demonstrate love and respect or hostility and disgust. We do not know the exact significance of each division-of-labor pattern, though we have found that certain patterns do have specific consequences. But we do know that work has deep meaning for identity and thus for difference, and that it articulates and supports sentimental relationships.

Riezler (1950) has said that sentiments like love require care and that care calls for work. A woman shows her love for husband and children by working to care for their needs for order, good food, and clean and mended clothes. A man shows his love for his family by providing them with money and security. Without care and its attendant work, Riezler felt that sentiments tend to be superficial. His ideas resemble those of Homans (1950), who maintained that sentiments arise through interaction, which is governed by work.

We add that both identity and difference depend on work.

Bott (1957) found that highly mobile couples who shared the house-work were confused about sex roles. Similarly, Hughes (1958) has repeatedly affirmed and demonstrated the links between work and identity. Only in work that is his own can a human test and find himself, and grow to be the self he aspires to be.

The family, like other parts of society, profits from the specialization permitted by a division of labor, and also from the clarification of responsibility and the greater motivation to work incidental to this kind of organization. If the husband and wife have distinct responsibilities, each can become skilled in certain tasks (for example, the wife in cooking and the husband in management of finances), derive pleasure from doing them well, and thus be motivated to good performance. If all tasks are shared, there is less chance for the development of skill, and no one can take the credit for good results, so motivation tends to decrease. There is much work to be done in a family, and the efficient completion of tasks and services is very important to the sense of well-being and security of the members.

The family with a culturally approved type of organization (division of labor and pattern of authority) is one in which the members feel culturally approved and rewarded. If the family varies from the approved model, its members experience their difference as a loss of approval or, more likely, as a sense of doing wrong or being peculiar. This loss of approval may not at first glance appear to be of importance. However, in view of the tremendous force of human striving for prestige and esteem and the significance of these rewards in the maintenance of a firm and positive ego identity, cultural values become an essential part of any consideration of the patterns of family organization. Of particular importance is their obvious impact on social status and mobility, which, in North American society, have become the most important measures of personal worth.

Authority is part of order and continuity, and its absence or weakness a mark of poor integration. The family, like all social groups, faces problems in the resolution of differences, in day-to-day decision making, and in the regulation of aggression. Most of these problems can be solved through discussion, and in modern urban families that no longer need strongly centralized authority and believe in equalitarianism, such a discursive and consultative orientation is optimal. Yet this does not eliminate the need for some system of authority, for conflicts must still be resolved, decisions made, and discipline maintained. We have found that modern urban families seem to be most successful when they adopt a system of authority that allows considerable discussion, but in cases of deadlock allocates the final decision to someone. Of course, the success of a particular form of authority depends also on its ability to meet the psychological and cultural needs of the family members.

But what is the importance of differences in the pattern of authority? We suggest several possibilities. First, for the family itself the existence of clear and responsible authority is necessary to planning, security, and smooth everyday functioning. If the parents are in conflict, or are weak and irresponsible, the work will be endless, the children poorly socialized, and the family crisis-prone. Second, if the pattern of authority is not congruent with what is culturally approved, the parents and children may be uneasy, and their roles and sexual identification may be in conflict with each other. There is reason to believe that authority, linked as it is to assertion and submission, is of importance in sexual gratification. In psychoanalytic theory, male assertiveness and potency go together, as do female submissiveness and receptiveness. We can assume that where authority is confused or role-reversed, it affects the sex life of the marriage partners. Finally, the patterns of authority reflect and affect the intrapsychic life and interaction of the family members.

Variations in the organization of the family result in different degrees of need satisfaction. This is illustrated in the effect of organizational variation on two widely accepted general needs: affection and sexuality.

Affection, or love, is not simply a matter of feeling, but also of demonstration. The ways in which people treat each other and care for each other sustain and demonstrate the affection between them. Homans's (1950) idea of the relationship between activities, interactions, and sentiments, and Riezler's (1950) idea of the relationship between work, care, and love provide theoretical explana-

tions for this. Different types of family organization may sustain
or dissipate various kinds of sentimental relationships. Our own
work has shown that the division of labor in the family strongly
affects such relationships, and that the husband and wife need both
shared and distinct responsibilities. Evidently, the sharing provides
the basis for common experiences and understanding, whereas the
distinct task areas provide the means for expressing care and demonstrating love, as well as for articulating the sexual identity of
each and the difference between them.

Since the need for sexuality includes both physical satisfaction and the need for a firm sexual identity, the differentiation of
tasks is relevant to sexuality in that it sustains differences in identity, which are important to physical satisfaction. Thus sexual attractiveness is to a considerable extent a matter of the possession of
the appropriate masculine or feminine traits, which include a wide
spectrum of activities. In North America masculine traits include
social status and success, and feminine traits certain expressive
skills. Within the family these appear in the expectation of a linkage between masculinity and decision making, and between femininity and encouragement of autonomy. These characteristics are
probably more important to heterosexual attractiveness than is
physical beauty. Masculinity or femininity is more a matter of
acting than being, and the appropriate forms of action are culturally defined. Our research findings strongly support these prem-
ises.

The interaction between psychodynamic needs and organization is a continuing reciprocal process. Psychodynamic needs can
shape organization, while organization certainly influences the pat-
terning of these needs. Our findings have impressed us with the
stability of family organization and the fact that, while psychodynamic changes certainly may occur, they do so at a gradual and
almost imperceptible pace. If one focuses on the ongoing transactional processes of the family, one gets the impression of fluidity,
but this fluidity occurs around a very stable base of organization
and psychodynamic needs.

According to the findings of this study, the kind of family
organization that is most viable and likely to produce emotionally

healthy children has a balanced division of labor, a father-led system of authority, a mother who is upwardly mobile, a respect for autonomy, strength in problem solving, and a husband and wife who thoroughly accept both their conjugal and parental roles. In the chapters that follow we analyze the relationship between each of these organizational elements and emotional health. Here we merely want to illustrate the effectiveness of a cluster of these elements in the prediction of the emotional health of the children. We have chosen work, power, and status for this purpose, since these elements were most amenable to rigorous measurement. Our findings show that, among the nine children of the three most viable families, seven were emotionally healthy and one was disturbed, while among the seventeen children of the five least viable families, none was healthy and twelve were disturbed.

The balanced, father-led family with an upwardly mobile mother appears to be the optimal pattern among middle-class Protestants. In the balanced family, the husband's participation is sufficient to provide him with a function within the family and a means of expressing his care and love for his wife and children; at the same time, sharing certain tasks helps him to understand and sympathize with his wife's problems and establishes a common basis of everyday experience. Within this pattern the work is divided in such a way that it can be done efficiently, with the responsibilities clearly established, so that each gains satisfaction from effective performance. It is a pattern rather expected from middle-class families of this generation, who still possess an idea of appropriate roles of husband and wife but expect a fair amount of sharing. Those who follow it have the added support of feeling that they are acting appropriately.

The father-led pattern of authority is in accordance with underlying psychodynamic concepts of the sex roles, particularly, male assertiveness and female receptiveness, and with social expectations of male and female relationships. Such a pattern of authority maintains sexual difference and supports the marriage partners' needs for a relationship in which they can be attracted to the other and feel themselves sexually attractive. At the same time, it contributes to a smoothly functioning family by permitting decisions

to be made and conflicts resolved. Finally, it is a pattern legiti-
mized by the norms of our society, which no longer approves of
patriarchy and condemns matriarchy. Its support by the community
thus provides the husband and wife with a sense of moral rectitude.

The upward mobility of the mother seems to strengthen her
respect for herself and for her husband and to produce satisfaction
with her role as wife and mother. We have speculated that the de-
creased prestige of the wife-mother role arising with its detachment
from a comprehensive kinship or tight community system makes
her depend almost entirely on the prestige that she derives from the
occupational prestige of her husband. In other words, in a social
system in which the members are increasingly dependent on objective, competitive sources of esteem, the wife's only chance for "success" is by making a good marriage. Her success in this venture is
reflected in her mobility scores.

Together, then, a balanced division of labor, father-led pattern of authority, and upwardly mobile mother lay the groundwork
for a satisfying and durable relationship between husband and wife.
The father, secure in his identity and position in the family, and
feeling warm and affectionate toward his wife, takes the initiative
in the solution of emotional problems. This initiative makes for
what we have called the problem-solving family. Our findings indicate that it is primarily the father who is responsible for this development. The mother is responsible for another important emotional condition—the encouragement and respect of the autonomy
of each family member. This, too, seems to be a product of her
sense of security and of being loved, which she translates into autonomy through her everyday relationship with her husband and
children.

All dimensions—a balanced division of labor, a father-led
pattern of authority, a capacity for the solution of emotional problems, and a high degree of autonomy—are related to the emotional
health of the children. This type of organization seems to maximize
satisfactions on the three levels of family experience, provide the
most positive husband-wife relationship and healthiest emotional
climate, and produce the emotionally healthiest children. In other
words, it makes for a viable family and viable personalities.

CHAPTER **3**

Who Are
the Healthy?

Emotional health is complex
and poorly defined, and its causes are even more complicated and
obscure. Thus it is necessary to limit the area to be studied and to
settle upon a definition of health. In the previous chapter we indicated that our search for causes was restricted to variations in the
organization of the family. In this chapter we describe our conception of emotional health and illness as well as the procedures and
criteria used to identify them.

Definitions of emotional health vary considerably. To place
our own ideas in perspective, we summarize the major points of
view. Although most serious definitions have been psychiatric, two

others must be disposed of first. One is the idea of the "normal" or "average." A person is usually regarded as normal if what he says and does conforms with certain standards laid down by the culture and social group to which he belongs. Eccentricity of behavior and even originality of thought are often regarded as abnormal. Furthermore, behavior acceptable to one status or age group or sex may not be acceptable to another. "Normal" behavior is thus an unsatisfactory measure of emotional health. Equally unsatisfactory is the statistical average. In psychiatry, particularly in the field of personality assessment, that which is statistically average is certainly not always healthy. Kinsey's (1953) disputed figures on orgasm in the female seem to show that a high percentage of women are rarely orgastic in intercourse, yet no psychiatrist would argue that this represents healthy functioning.

The second idea is that emotional health is simply "adjustment," or passive acceptance of environmental conditions. We cannot accept this. Health implies a state of surplus energy, vitality, and awareness, as well as active attempts by an individual to master his environment. The healthy individual does more than adapt to his surroundings; he makes them adjust to him as well.

In defining emotional health and illness, psychiatrists seem to have adopted one, or a combination, of the following emphases: feeling and behavior, unconscious dynamic material and the relationship between the conscious and unconscious, or the actualization of inner potentials. The first is illustrated in a definition by Freud, who, when asked what he thought a normal, healthy person should do well, replied "Love and work." It is a simple but useful definition, since both love and work are intricate phenomena; moreover, it can be applied transculturally. Menninger's (1946) definition is similar. He states, "Let us define mental health as the adjustment of human beings to the world and each other with a maximum of effectiveness and happiness. Not just efficiency, or just contentment, or the grace of obeying the rules of the game cheerfully. It is all of these together. It is the ability to maintain an even temper and a happy disposition. This, I think, is a healthy mind."

According to Fromm (1941), "The term *normal* or *healthy* can be defined in two ways. Firstly, from the standpoint of functioning society, one can call a person normal or healthy if he is able to fulfill the social role he is to take in that given society. Secondly, from the standpoint of the individual, we look upon health or normalcy as the optimum of growth and happiness of the individual." The Expert Committee on Mental Health of the World Health Organization has defined mental health as "the capacity to establish harmonious interpersonal relationships."

The second approach, stressing the concern with unconscious conflicts and the relationship between the conscious and unconscious, derives from classical psychoanalysis and is probably the most widespread. Thus Kubie (1954) states that healthy behavior results "whenever an alliance of the conscious and unconscious systems predominates" in the production of that behavior. "Such behavior never becomes either insatiable or stereotyped. It can be altered by the experience of success and failure, of reward and punishment, or pleasure and pain. . . . It is, therefore, anchored in reality, yet it remains freely flexible."

Hartmann (1939) conceives of emotional health in a different way. He mentions the apparent conflict between the two long-held psychoanalytic concepts of emotional health as instinctual freedom and as rational behavior. He disposes of this seeming conflict by stating that "the rational must incorporate the irrational as an element in its design." He emphasizes freedom, which on one level is "control exercised by means of the conscious and preconscious ego," and on another, the condition in which a healthy ego can allow some of its functions, including "freedom," to be put out of action occasionally, abandoning itself to "compulsion" (central control).

The emphasis on actualization of inner potentials is illustrated by Maslow's (1954) theory that "basic human needs are organized into a hierarchy of relative prepotency." This theory implies that gratification is just as important as deprivation in motivation, since it releases the organism from the domination of first physiological, then basic psychological needs, permitting the emergence of more social goals. The physiological and psychological needs and their partial goals, when chronically gratified, cease to exist as active determinants or organizers of behavior. Thus, according to Maslow, freedom from the pressing demands of these basic human needs enables man more completely to actualize his innate potential because it makes available the libidinal energy otherwise devoted to defense mechanisms. "Full health and normal and desirable development consist in actualizing man's inner inherent nature and potentials."

In the past, classical psychoanalysis offered little information on emotional health, as opposed to illness. Maslow (1954) states "the science of psychology has been far more successful on a negative than on the positive side; it has revealed to us much about man's shortcomings, his illnesses, his sins, but little about his potentialities, his virtue, his achievable aspirations, or his full psychological height. It is as if psychology had voluntarily restricted itself to only half its rightful jurisdiction and that the darker, meaner half. This is no extrinsic, superficial attitude; it seems clear rather that it is intrinsic and at the heart of the whole culture."

Fortunately, the development of ego theory as put forth by Hartmann (1939), Erikson (1959), and others has done much to rectify the deficiency. Early psychoanalytic theory attempted to explain all behavior in terms of basic instinctual drives and the defenses against them. It was concerned with the id and confined to the internal experiences of the person. Ego theory enlarges the area of concern by also considering the strengths and weaknesses derived from special noninstinctual capacities like intelligence, and from the ways in which the person has learned to deal with and integrate his emotions, intrapsychic conflicts, and social emotional relationships. This theory helps us to understand man's adaptation to reality.

RATING SCHEMA

The philosophy underlying our rating schema is that an understanding of emotional health and illness should be based on standards of performance derived from studies of the needs and capacities of the human organism. The value judgment inherent in our schema is that emotional health involves the optimal utilization of the innate potentials and functions of that organism. It is similar to the judgments expressed by such workers as Maslow (1954) and Rado (1961).

Our schema can be applied transculturally; it evades the trap of "cultural relativity," which holds that emotional health varies directly with the culture and that there may be many different types. Though there are many modes of pathological and healthy personality adjustments, we do not accept the theory that there are various kinds of health. We believe that the human organism, with its inherent potentials and functions, is universal, and that health depends on the optimal realization of capacities. Obviously, there are many cultures and subcultures that do not permit such full realization, but this should not be used to refute the basic definition. If a culture constricts the development of human capacities, it is, in our view, inimical to emotional health.

Since many, if not all, societies are in some way inimical to emotional health, the potentially healthy man in such surroundings is faced with certain alternatives. (1) He could make active attempts to change the environment. Unless, however, the frustrations that he felt were widely shared, he would be unsuccessful. Probably all he could do would be to change his immediate environment, such as the family or peer group. This might require such a withdrawal from the larger environment that he could no longer be said to be adapting to or participating in it, and the result would be similar to that of the other alternatives. (2) He could escape to an environment that would be conducive to healthy functioning. (3) He could resort to the choice perhaps most frequent: the development of pathological psychic distortions that allow a less consciously painful adjustment. In this context Hartmann (1939) has noted: "The nature of the environment may be such that a pathological development of the psyche offers a more satisfactory solution than would a healthy one."

In evaluating the degree of emotional health or illness in our subjects we used three general criteria developed in the works of Erikson (1950) and Jahoda (1955, 1958): (1) structured psychiatric symptoms, (2) social and occupational adaptation, and (3) psychodynamic integration.

By structured psychiatric symptoms we mean phobias; gross depression and anxiety; hallucinations; delusions; hypochrondriacal complaints; symptoms of organic brain disorder; feelings of depersonalization, unreality, and dissociation; perversions and addictions; symptoms and signs of the illnesses commonly accepted as "psychosomatic" conditions, such as migraine, some forms of asthma and allergy, some forms of eczematous dermatitis, essential hypertension, ulcerative colitis, and peptic ulcer. Our experience indicates that the presence of structured psychiatric symptoms signals the existence of a fairly advanced process of personality decompensation with considerable underlying psychopathology.

The criterion of social and occupational adaptation takes into consideration some of the points raised by Jahoda (1955, 1958), who wrote that an individual's emotional health represented "active adjustment or attempt at mastery of his environment as distinct both from his inability to adjust and from his indiscriminate acceptance of environmental conditions." It is also related to the World Health Organization's (WHO) definition of mental health as "the capacity to establish harmonious interpersonal relationships."

In evaluating the capacity of the individual to establish a positive level of adaptation in the sociocultural and occupational spheres of existence, particular attention is paid to whether or not he is utilizing his inner potentials optimally. The quality of his interpersonal relationships and of his occupational commitment is also evaluated, and his sociocultural environment examined to determine whether it is congenial to the development of a positive level of social and occupational adaptation.

Whereas the first two criteria of our rating schema are almost self-explanatory, the third—psychodynamic integration—requires detailed elaboration. This criterion consists of two major components: the structural-functional and the psychodynamic-motivational.

The structural-functional component refers to the various structural and functional elements that enter into the development and operation of the human personality. These elements include perception, apperception, cognition and intellect, affect, and the body functions, including sexuality. In a state of positive emotional health or psychodynamic integration all these elements are expected to be present at or above a certain minimum level of potential, to be functioning at approximately an optimum level, and to be in harmonious balance. The psychodynamic-motivational component refers to the conscious and unconscious psychic conflicts, or "crisis stages," that each individual must deal with during life development and the process of everyday living. In a state of emotional health and psychodynamic integration these conflicts are dealt with satisfactorily without undue anxiety.

The first element of the structural-functional component is perception; *optimal perception* is the ability to perceive oneself and the reality world around one accurately. Individuals do so with varying degrees of constriction and distortion, which may block their awareness and knowledge of the reality around and inside them. Some individuals may perceive the world about them with clarity but shut off the awareness of anything occurring inside them. Conversely, some become so preoccupied with what goes on inside them that outer perceptions are screened out. The psychotic person is the classic extreme example. The paranoid schizophrenic often sees his world as being set up in some special way to attack, destroy, or defeat him. He misconstrues the messages coming from within rather grossly, and he may even see himself as someone else —Napoleon, say, or God. Most, if not all, individuals constrict and distort their world to some degree; the emotionally healthy individuals are those who do so to a minimum degree, if at all.

The healthy students in our study could give a multidimensional description of their parents, so that a fairly clear picture of them as individuals in their own right emerged. At the same time, they could depict their own feelings, responses, and roles in relation to their parents. We found that the level of emotional health of the individual students varied directly with the clarity, richness, breadth, and depth of their descriptions of both parents and their interaction with them.

The answers of the emotionally unhealthy students differed from those of the emotionally healthy in quality, quantity, and content. The emotionally unhealthy usually gave very brief statements, loaded with clichés and the standard "answers"; then followed anxiety-laden blocking in speech and inability to go any further. "Father——He is a good father——He works hard——

[block]——Do you want to know what he looks like?——He is a fine father. Mother——a typical mother——She's very good to us ——easy to get along with——[block]——I guess that's all I can say." The students giving such answers could rarely give any description of significant interaction between themselves and their parents, nor admit to having had at any time unfavorable feelings toward them. Some rambled on at length about their parents without saying anything, giving answers that were cliché-ridden, irrelevant, repetitive, shallow, and empty of significant content.

Occasional students seemed to be able to give a fair description of one parent but almost nothing about the other, indicating emotional conflict with the latter severe enough to interfere with apperception of him. One male student, who had a very intense relationship with his mother and was highly identified with her, seemed able to go on indefinitely, giving a minutely detailed and excellent description of her, but was unable to say more than a few words about his father.

Cognition and intelligence constitute a second element of the structural-functional component. In a state of emotional health we expect the cognitive processes of the individual and the function called intelligence to be operating clearly and around the level of optimum potential. The capacity to associate, to think abstractly, and to conceptualize ideas with more or less sophistication should be observable. We expect the emotionally healthy individual to be able to think rationally and logically and to function at or near the level of his innate intellectual endowment.

Degree of native endowment and educational level are two important variables in this functioning. Emotional health requires that an individual have at least enough intelligence to maintain himself throughout life without undue dependence on others. Since the healthy person is one who functions at a level commensurate with his intelligence, even one with an IQ as low as 80 would certainly be considered healthy if he does indeed function at that level. Obviously, too, the level and quality of his education, as well as the intellectual stimulation given him in his family, directly influence the effectiveness with which an individual utilizes his cognitive and intellectual resources.

Affective functioning is our third element of the structural-functional component. Most humans are potentially capable of exhibiting a broad spectrum of affect in intrapsychic and interpersonal functioning. These feelings can be divided into the emergency emotions, which include fear, rage, guilt, sorrow, and depression, and the welfare emotions, which include pleasure, joy, happiness, tenderness, love, and pride.

Unless an individual is capable of both feeling and exhibiting this spectrum, he is functioning psychopathologically. Some people may be capable of feeling and being aware of these affects, but unable to express them appropriately in their relationships with others. Others may habitually suppress the overt expression of these emotions, and this too is considered psychopathological if there are no rational reasons for it. In our society most people show psychopathology in the ability to express rage openly and directly and in the experiencing and expression of the softer feelings of love and tenderness. The latter is particularly marked among males, who feel it is not manly to feel, particularly to display, affection.

Some people demonstrate easily and vitally a wide range of affects; others seem placid, flat, and limited. In evaluating the latter, environmental stimulation must be considered and care must be taken to distinguish the following types: (1) those whose affective endowment is limited as a result of infantile developmental traumata, such as early maternal deprivation, or some other gross difficulty in the mother-child dyad (in the case of the schizotypal individual in whom there is total or partial failure of development of the welfare emotions, Rado (1960) postulates a presently unknown genetic defect); (2) those who, though fully endowed, are never able to achieve a satisfactory integration of affective functioning because of difficulties in their early intrafamilial relationships; (3) those who are fully endowed and have achieved satisfactory integration of their potentials, but who appear to be overly placid or limited in affective range. We encountered many such individuals in screening the adolescents in the study. Investigation revealed them as capable of a wide range of deep and appropriate responses, but slower than others to react, and lacking in sparkle, though they were in no way depressed in the usual sense of the

term. This pattern seemed to be related to a family environment
that was lacking in vitality or emotional stimulation. There were no
marked conflicts in these families, but their lives were more narrow
and constricted than those of most of our families.

By our criteria, the individuals classified in the first and
second groups were rated as demonstrating considerable pathology
in the affective sphere. Those in the third group were rated as
healthy, but not as healthy as subjects enjoying intact and integrated affective functioning with more vitality and force.

Body functioning is a fourth element of the structural-functional component. The body must be healthy if it is to satisfy psy-
chobiological needs. Clinical and research evidence demonstrates
that good physical health is requisite to psychic well-being. Similarly, psychic difficulties and conflicts are often expressed in mal-
function of one or more body systems. Thus, for example, emotional conflicts related to sexuality frequently result in impotence
or frigidity; conversely, injury to the sexual end organs can wreak
havoc in the psyche.

The structural-functional component represents only half of
the psychodynamic integration criterion; the other half is the psychodynamic-motivational component. Our schema includes the assessment of psychodynamic and motivational factors in the overall
rating system. This inclusion complicates the rating process, since
with phenomenological material one ordinarily uses direct inspection, whereas with motivational and psychodynamic material it is
necessary to add reported introspection and inference. The addition is necessary because psychodynamic motivation most often expresses itself at an unconscious or nonreporting level, but it in-
creases the difficulties inherent in achieving reliability and validity
in psychosocial research.

The evaluation of the conscious and unconscious aspects of
psychodynamic motivation and their role in the psychodynamic
integration of the individual requires a sound knowledge of the
science of basic psychodynamics and considerable clinical experience in its application. The science of psychodynamics is based
largely on the findings of Freud, with the additions and modifica-
tions of the many followers who have made significant contribu-

tions. Prominent among those who have been most helpful to us are Rado, Kardiner, Hartmann, Erikson, and Ackerman.

In this phase of our study we found the work of Erikson (1950, 1959) especially helpful. Erikson's model of personality development, which is based upon a progression of developmental stages, expresses "the unity of the human life cycle and the specific dynamics of each of its stages, as presented by the laws of individual development and of social organization." This model is an outgrowth of Freud's theory of psychosexual stages of personality development, which Erikson develops much further in an attempt "to bridge the theory of infantile sexuality and our knowledge of the child's physical and social growth within his family and social structure." He states that each stage is a period of decisive and critical development of a distinct component of mental health: There is "a progression through time of a differentiation of parts. This indicates (1) that each item of the healthy personality to be discussed is systematically related to all others, and that they all depend on the proper development in the proper sequence of each item; (2) that each item exists in some form before 'its' decisive and critical time normally arrives . . . each [component] comes to its ascendance, meets its crisis, and finds its lasting solution toward the end of the stages mentioned."

Each distinct component of mental health that is dealt with at any given stage has a sort of negative counterpart, and a balance between the positive and negative components is attained at each stage. Erikson points out very carefully that one of the chief misuses of his schema has been the interpretation that at each stage the positive component being dealt with is an achievement, secured once and for all. He indicates quite clearly that "the negative senses [of the components] are and remain the dynamic counterpart of the positive senses throughout life. What the child acquires at a given stage is a certain ratio between the positive and the negative which, if the balance is toward the positive, will help him to meet later crises with a better chance for unimpaired total development." He cautions against the development of "the idea that at any stage a *goodness* is achieved which is impervious to new conflicts within and changes without."

Erikson's stages of development and the positive and negative components at each stage are:

1. Basic trust versus basic mistrust, which stage occurs in about the first year of life.
2. Autonomy versus shame and doubt, which occurs in about the second and third years.
3. Initiative versus guilt, which occurs in about the fourth and fifth years.
4. Industry versus inferiority, which occurs during latency—that is, from about the sixth year until early adolescence.
5. Identity versus identity diffusion, which occurs during adolescence.
6. Intimacy and distantiation versus self-absorption, which occurs during the first stage of adulthood.
7. Generativity versus stagnation, which occurs during the middle stage of adulthood.
8. Integrity versus despair and disgust, which occurs during the last stage of adulthood.

Our view is that an emotionally healthy individual is not one who does not have conflicts; rather he is one who has dealt and is dealing in a satisfactory manner with the conflicts inherent in each stage of development. To paraphrase Erikson, he has acquired at each stage a ratio between the positive and the negative components of mental health whose balance is toward the positive. Such a ratio helps the individual meet later crises with a better chance of unimpaired total development.

In assessing the psychodynamic and motivational aspects of psychodynamic integration, we focused on how the individual had dealt with the developmental stages and periods of crisis through which he had passed at the time of evaluation. We did this by means of the psychiatric interview and the projective techniques of the Rorschach and TAT tests.

In the psychiatric interview we attempted to obtain: a cross-sectional view of the subject's functioning in all areas at the time of investigation, and a longitudinal view of the psychogenetic development from birth. We utilized the direct inspectional powers of the subject and the interviewer plus inferential reasoning on our part based upon the reported direct observations and introspective thinking of the subject. Our knowledge of psychodynamics enabled us to deal with material from both the conscious (reporting) and unconscious (nonreporting) levels of the subject's psyche. Using these findings, we assessed the way in which the subject had dealt with his emotional conflicts and crises. In the case of adolescent subjects, we attempted to assess the following:

1. How is the subject dealing with the problem of identity development? Is he dealing with it actively and moving toward some degree of satisfactory resolution, or is he failing?

2. Has the individual developed a sense of industry, as Erikson uses the term? Has he developed a sense of being useful, of being able to do and produce things, and to feel the pleasure of work completed, or does he harbor a sense of inadequacy?

3. Has the subject developed initiative? Does he have a sense of having the right, ability, and freedom to decide what he wants to become, or does he feel defeated, with a resultant sense of guilt over his inner secret wishes?

4. Has the subject developed a feeling of autonomy? Does he have a sense of his own uniqueness as an individual separate from others and under his own control, or is he laden with shame and doubt, feeling that he is still merged with his parents and subject to their complete control?

5. Has the subject developed the ability to trust and to expect some good from others, or is he laden with mistrust, expecting nothing but harm from his social environment?

6. Is the subject coming to grips with his sexual drives or not?

Empirical findings indicate that failure to attain satisfactory psychodynamic integration generates anxiety and that the degree of anxiety—conscious and unconscious—is directly correlated with the degree of impairment of integration and concomitant psychopathology.

On the basis of our criteria of symptoms, adaptation, and integration, we set up four categories ranging from emotional health to illness:

A. Absence of structured psychiatric symptoms; social and occupational adaptation; dynamic integration.

B. Absence of structured psychiatric symptoms; social and occupational adaptation; mild impairment of dynamic integration with mild anxiety.

C. Absence of structured psychiatric symptoms; social or occupational maladaptation; moderate impairment of dynamic integration with moderate psychopathology and moderate anxiety.

D. Presence of structured psychiatric symptoms; social and occupational maladaptation; severe psychopathology and severe anxiety.

For individual evaluations each of these categories was broken down into subcategories, so that we had, for example, A-1, A-2, and A-3. In general, individuals falling into Categories A and B were emotionally healthy, while those falling into C and D were emotionally disturbed. However, we decided that Category C-1 should be considered a neutral or intermediate category, since in fact it seems to be a mixture of the borderline healthy and borderline disturbed.

In our assessments the normal procedure was to look first for structured psychiatric symptoms that would automatically put the individual into Category D. If they were not present, we sought evidence of social or occupational maladaptation, which normally placed the individual into Category C. If neither of these two symptoms was present, the analysis of dynamic integration was used as the final test of emotional health. However, before the final decision was reached, each case was reviewed in terms of the three criteria.

Judgments based on these criteria were made by the psychiatrist, using interview data, and by the psychologist, using TAT and Rorschach results. The rank-order correlation between the two sets of judgments was plus .75, which is better than the .01 level of probability. When there was disagreement, the ratings of the two judges were averaged, except where these ratings were in adjoining categories; then a final judgment was reached after a case conference, which also included the sociologist. The ninety-six subjects were rated as follows: A (very healthy), one; B (healthy), nineteen; C (somewhat disturbed), sixty-six; and D (very disturbed), ten. That the majority of our subjects fell into Category C is understandable, since those in that category demonstrated varying degrees of character neuroses or ego distortion. These were the people who are frequently spoken of as "well-adjusted," primarily because they show no structured psychiatric symptoms.

Since these general categories were subdivided into three each, we had twelve ratings ranging from the highest level of emotional health (12) to the lowest (1). Both the psychiatrist and the psychologist rated the degree of emotional health of each subject according to the twelve-point schema. Variations in this continuum were then rank-order correlated with a large number of family and personality variables. For purposes of cross-tabulation we divided the children into three categories, calling the rating from 12 to 7 "healthy," the rating of 6 "intermediate," and the ratings of from 5 to 1 "disturbed." In dividing the parents of our subjects, since the distribution seemed heavily biased toward illness, we called 12 to 6 "healthy," 5 "intermediate," and 4 to 1 "disturbed." However, the reader should keep in mind that though the cutting points in these continua reflected the judgment of the psychiatric director, the continua, reflecting good or poor emotional health, can stand by themselves.

Some question of tautological reasoning might be raised about the emotional health evaluations, as it might about any system of clinical evaluation. The clinician always views each symptom or criterion in terms of what he already knows about the subject; that is, the symptom is seen in terms of the whole man. The evaluation is a Gestalt one. This is both the strength and weakness of clinical judgments, and both were naturally involved in our own psychiatric clinical judgments, and, to a lesser degree, our psychological evaluations. This raises serious problems about the degree to which the study validates its criteria of emotional health. Consequently, we have made no claims of validation and restricted our dependent variable to gross evaluations of emotional health and illness.

There are a number of reasons why these gross distinctions are probably valid. First, we exercised great care to make certain

that the ratings of the psychiatrist and the psychologists were absolutely independent and, as far as possible, based on different kinds
of data. There was a very high degree of agreement between the
emotional health ratings of these two professional judges. Second,
the distribution of emotional health and illness in our sample population closely approximates that found in other major serious studies. Finally, for most parts of data analysis we collapsed our ratings
into three general categories—Healthy, Intermediate, and Disturbed—on the assumption that thereby we would insure an absolute difference in emotional health between the extremes.

BEHAVIORAL CORRELATES

The degree to which a family participated in activities involving others, such as community services, social sports, and visiting, was definitely related to the emotional health of the mother.
We found a significant positive correlation between her emotional
health and the extent to which she participated in such activities
(r equals plus .379, n 54), she and her husband participated (r
equals plus .428, n 55), and the whole family participated (r
equals plus .401, n 54).

The relationship between emotional health and social experiences is probably a reciprocal one in which a person's health
tends to make him sociable and his social experiences reinforce his
health. Apparently, this is particularly true of the housewife, whose
role is held in such low esteem that she needs the emotional support
of outside activities. However, to break away and seek outside support, she must already have an extra degree of emotional strength.

We obtained extensive data on the degree to which our
subjects participated in activities during high school. There was a
large range, and participation within this range varied with the
emotional health ratings. Some students reported almost no participation in school activities, while others had been extremely active.
We decided to rate their activity as low if they listed three or fewer
activities and indicated that they did not participate very heavily
in these, and high if they listed seven or more activities and indicated that their participation in some was heavy, involving, for
example, frequent attendance of meetings or office-holding. A high

scorer gave the following record: Boy Scouts, two years; Y.M.C.A., one year; editor of school paper; student council; football, basketball, volleyball; dance committee; school play; athletic council; ski club. In contrast, a low scorer said that he had joined no clubs or organizations while in high school, though he had played in the school band and participated in interclass sports.

There is statistically significant association between emotional health and the participation in high school activities. Almost all the healthy children were high participators.

Most of the disturbed parents (eleven out of fourteen disturbed men and ten out of twelve disturbed women) had intercourse less than four times a month, while the emotionally healthy parents (four out of nine men and seven out of ten women) had intercourse more often. The details of this relationship are presented in Chapter Eight. Here we simply note that frequency of intercourse is an excellent behavioral indicator of disturbance, if not of health.

The healthy subjects seemed to be able to respond with, and display in appropriate contexts, the full spectrum of human affects. They seemed to be in touch with their feelings and behaved accordingly. The unhealthy subjects seemed out of touch with certain kinds of affect; many displayed a generalized affective constriction. They showed a marked level of affective poverty and flatness, which was not due to depression, for these symptoms were absent, but simply to their emotional barrenness.

Nearly all of the disturbed subjects had problems in the expression of rage. They seemed afraid of the overt expression of anger, and most had to deny the existence of it inside themselves.

Every one of our adolescent subjects was extremely well behaved and controlled. Indeed, there is evidence that many of them suffered from overcontrol. This group certainly did not confirm the allegation that modern adolescents are nothing but impulse-ridden, gratification-seeking, uncontrolled animals.

The sexual mores of the students were so conservative that it was somewhat difficult to evaluate their response to their sexual drives. We focused on the manner in which they dealt with their sexual feelings and fantasies, since there was surprisingly little sex-

ual behavior to evaluate. The students participated in a minimum
of petting and kissing.

In this sphere we evaluated as healthy the individuals who
were able to remain in touch with their sexual feelings and fantasies, even though they chose for their own reasons not to act on
them. These individuals were able to accept their sexuality and to
recognize their sexual feelings and fantasies as pleasant or at times,
perhaps, disturbing or frightening. We evaluated as unhealthy those
who, as a result of their fear, were forced to deny their impulses
and fantasies, or to label them as bad and consequently to feel extreme conscious or unconscious guilt over them.

Many of the unhealthy subjects tended to project this guilt,
that is, they felt that anyone who had sexual feelings and desires
was bad and unclean. This attitude seemed more common among
the boys. It was interesting to listen to these adolescent males express such prudish, mid-Victorian views on sex with such strong
feeling. The need to reject their sexuality undoubtedly interfered
with their achievement of satisfactory sexual identification, as shown
by the fact that as a group they displayed more difficulty in this
than did the healthy subjects.

Because these adolescents were so anxiety-laden in the area
of sexuality, we felt unsure of our evaluations. At times we felt that
the best we could do was to make an educated guess. It will be
easier to evaluate their sexual functioning in a few years' time,
following more opportunity for experience. It seems likely that the
anxiety and rigidity surrounding their sexuality were reinforced by
their living at home with their families, which were all middle-
class, with the usual bourgeois sexual mores. If the students had
been living away from home among peers, they might have experi-
mented more freely.

On life aims and goals and ego identity, we rated as healthy
those who indicated that they could and did grapple actively with
the issues. As a group the students were quite vague and hazy
about life goals; they seemed not to give them much thought. In
the healthy subjects this seemed to be a simple consequence of in-
ertia and lack of environmental stimulation, whereas in the disturbed subjects it was complicated by anxiety that seriously inter-

fered with their willingness and ability to deal with what issues did arise. These individuals did not seem to dream and fantasy about the future and their place in it. When they did so, their images were staid, safe, and uninspired. Except in rare instances, it seemed that even in their fantasies they could not allow themselves to reach for the stars.

The healthier students showed they were capable of giving some thought to the future and had in fact already done so. The boys usually indicated a desire to work in a general field such as business or engineering or in some specific scientific discipline such as chemistry or physics. They thought primarily in terms of security, mentioning that they would want jobs with large companies that had good security plans. Their aims seemed to be geared toward the life of a middle-level executive with a wife and several children and a house in the suburbs. They appeared not to aspire beyond the mold created by their fathers. Their choice of occupation seemed to be only a means to an end—not something to be enjoyed. The healthy girls usually indicated that they wanted some career, such as nursing, teaching, or physiotherapy, for a short period, and then marriage and a family. Here also the ring of commitment and conviction was missing.

The less healthy students showed much more vagueness and confusion about future goals. Their anxiety about themselves and their future seemed to make it very difficult for them to grapple with such problems. As one disturbed youngster put it, "I don't like to set any definite future. I like it to come about as it is going to. I don't like to set anything definite. I don't like to think things are going to turn out cut and dried. I hope I can reach the point that when the crises and disappointments come along I can face them somehow." When these individuals did give statements concerning their future goals, they were usually shallow and stereotyped. When the disturbed girls were asked for further associations, many said, after long periods of blocking, "oh yes——of course I'll want to get married——maybe, of course, children and all that."

In the area of ego identity there was a marked difference between the healthy and the disturbed. The healthy students had obviously managed to develop some inner sense of self that was

congruent with the world about them. Some were more articulate
and sensitive about identity than others, yet all were capable of
demonstratitng that they were developing a sense of identity.

The findings were quite different for the disturbed students.
Many were incapable of giving an objective description of any
sense of self. "I'm just an average person——that's all." "Just an
ordinary person. . . ." And many displayed marked blocking in
response to the request for a description of self. This was punctu-
ated with "I don't know——this is so difficult. . . ." Some gave a
superficial description of their physical characteristics and were
then unable to say more.

In the interviews with the adult subjects, our findings were
almost the same as those described with the students. We felt that
the adults had a greater tendency than the students to withhold
information on matters that they found difficult to discuss, such as
sexuality. Nevertheless, because of their sincerity and their strong
conscious desire to cooperate, the effect of this tendency was negli-
gible.

CHAPTER 4

Functions and Relationships

The family is perhaps more than anything else a unit of interacting personalities (Burgess and Locke, 1945)—a system of emotions and interlocking needs on the deepest level. Both child and adult must look to the family for most of their emotional satisfaction. It is axiomatic in Freudian theory and in many theories of personality that the child's personality is formed in the context of his earliest relationships with his parents, and particularly with his mother. His needs are said to be given a voice in that first conversation of emotions, and it is this voice that gives the directions through much of the rest of his life. We accept these ideas, though we would note certain limitations.

57

Psychodynamic theory grew on the memories of people in therapy. Consequently, it came to view the personality as the idiosyncratic product of the special relationships of the individual with emotionally important others. The patient's impassioned relationships with his mother and father, as seen through his eyes, constituted a persuasive explanation of his pathology, and even today there are many who remain committed to this view. It was some time before the patient's specialized view of his family universe was questioned. True, no psychoanalyst was ever naive enough to accept what the patient remembered and said at face value; one purpose of their work together was to assist the patient to unravel his own distortions. Yet these early psychoanalytic researchers remained limited by the patient's view, which even in its most valid perceptions could only be a point of view. Not until recent years did therapists begin to look at the family itself. A consequence of this change, which has a long and fascinating history, was the recognition of the family as a system of emotional relationships that is reflected in the child's personality.

The emotional system that characterizes a particular family begins with the marriage of two personalities. The bride and groom both bring to this newly formed relationship their own needs, expressive forms, images of relationship, and sociocultural expectations. These are seldom the same for both, but they are usually related. In some way each finds in the marriage partner some part of his self and some answer to his needs for security, dominance, nurturance, or submission. These are but names in our chaotic vocabulary for human needs, but no matter what words we use to describe them, it is likely that these needs enter into the marriage.

Some students of the family (Winch, 1955) have found that most husbands and wives marry because of reciprocal, or complementary, needs. However, the relationship between their needs is seldom perfect. It is apparent that there is much marital conflict stemming from power struggles, clashing dependencies, claims, and rejections. Claims, or needs, of the partners play an important part in the persistence of their marriage and their satisfaction in it. One must not assume, however, that because the marriage persists, these problems are resolved. The struggles and tensions may persist throughout a lifetime, often ramifying into the parents' relationships with the children.

The task might be easier if the married couple were completely free to seek an adjustment that would meet their needs, but this is almost never the case. Even if their separate needs can be adjusted, the partners are likely to find that there are demands outside themselves and their relationship that must also be satisfied; and the demands of the social group, community, or culture may actually conflict with the adjustment the couple is trying to make. A familiar example is role reversal, in which the husband is submissive and prefers the expressive role, while his wife is hard and dominating. Though the couple will probably seek a more modest variation of the theme, the husband may want to stay home and take care of the house, the wife to go to work. Should they do so, their marital relationship is bound to be affected by the community's disapproval, whether or not they have internalized the culture's role definitions. Furthermore, their demands for conformity will change with age, the coming of children, health, and socioeconomic status. So even if they do make an adjustment, it is bound to be unstable.

The tenor of this discussion might be taken to be that all marriages are in a constant state of crisis. In fact a prominent Canadian sociologist once defined the family in exactly these terms, as a collective process of meeting one crisis after another (Dawson, 1952). We feel that this point of view must be included in a discussion of the family. Yet we recognize that it distorts the fundamental stability of the arrangements that are usually worked out— that is, the routines that bind family life, or the traditional ways of treating and doing things that most families develop. This basic stability of family life is a necessity if the family is to survive and meet the needs of its members, even partially. Any group of people living together must, in order to achieve cooperation, be able to anticipate each other's responses and predict each other's behavior, and in order for this to take place, there must be routines and stability. In a sense, all families are marked by some kind of stability, though it may be exceedingly fragile. Ordinarily, when the relationship that meets the needs of the husband and wife also meets

the needs of the family as a social group, as well as the expectations of the society, the family arrangements are durable. To the
extent that this is not the case, they tend to be fragile.

There is yet another way in which the family must meet
the demands of its members for the expression of general human
needs. It may well be that the family's capacity to permit its members to develop and express the range of human emotions is what
ultimately marks its success or failure. The family must be able to
permit and to contain the expression of emotions like fear, rage,
sadness, love, and jealousy. Whether it can do so depends on the
arrangements the members have set up to accommodate their psychological and sociocultural demands. Some families cannot permit
the expression of rage, and it works like a gangrene into all the
fibers of family life. Others permit but cannot control it, and it cuts
like a scythe. Still other families do not seem to be able to express
tenderness. When only one side of emotional life is expressed, one
should be suspicious, for emotions are complementary. Affection
without hostility is not real affection, but a shallow and empty
thing, and perhaps even a masked form of what it denies. Families
who deny any part of their emotions are certainly lopsided, and
may produce emotionally crippled children.

In the sense that the family unit is a response to these various pressures, we can think of it as a struggle for equilibrium, or
an attempt to reach some form of organization that meets at least
the minimal needs of its individual members for psychodynamic adjustment, and of the group for organizational efficiency and community acceptance. When the organization of the family is such
that it does meet these diverse pressures, the family environment is
usually stable and healthy.

We do not suggest that there is only one form of organization that satisfies these criteria, for obviously there is much variation. However, we would point out that a given culture lays down
criteria that limit variation, that the functional prerequisites of a
small group's organization impose other limitations, and finally,
that the general emotional and biological needs of the members are
usually fairly standard. Hence within a particular culture it is probable that there will be a form of organization that is optimal.

What is generally optimal, of course, may for some be impractical. People must live with their personalities, whatever their deficiencies, and many are forced by the needs of their special personalities to seek marital relationships that pose difficulties. Fortunately, most of these relationships have considerable survival value, permitting the members of the family to lead useful and often pleasant lives, though not without strain, sacrifice, or even crippling. However, because a family can maintain the façade of harmony and continue to exist does not mean that there are satisfaction and happiness. Many families that are torn by strife and hatred, and whose members are sick, miserable, and lonely, continue to persist and to look respectable. In fact it is often true that people stick together because they are too sick and weak and frightened to do anything about their troubles or because of their psychopathological needs for each other.

The members of a family may display frantic efforts to cling to their problems when these are threatened by therapeutic intervention or other changes. This is a recurrent problem of the psychotherapist who works with children. A child may be brought to the clinic because of some outside interference like the school or the police, or because his psychological problems have shown up in symptoms that are embarrassing to the family. But often the family strongly resists a basic change in the child. As soon as basic personality and behavioral changes begin to occur, the parents seek to remove the child from therapy or otherwise sabotage its progress. This is because any change in the sick child's functioning makes it difficult, if not impossible, for the family to maintain its existing pattern of relationships. For instance, the child might be ill because both the mother and father had scapegoated him, heaping upon him the anger they felt toward each other. If after therapy the child no longer accepted this anger, or if the therapist prevented the parents from venting it on the child, they might turn it on themselves or each other, with the result of either breaking up the family or creating new relationships and a new equilibrium. Family-centered therapy is designed to help the family meet its crises with adaptive changes in its system of relationships.

Having described the three areas of pressure that mold the

psychosocial organization of the family, and suggested that two of the areas—the social and cultural—are relatively stable and fixed, we shall describe our theories and findings concerning the psychodynamic organization of the family. However, we caution that though we describe this organization by itself, it is in fact always a part of, and to some extent explained by, the social organization of the family, and some of its most important consequences arise through its effects on the social organization.

When we speak of the psychodynamic organization of the family, we are referring to the emotional, or affective, content of the roles played by each member and the meaning of these roles to the other members. These roles are shaped by the responses of the family members to each other. Thus the way in which the son is expected to act will be shaped by the rewards he received from his parents for acting in certain ways (passively or assertively) and the punishments he received for acting in others.

The way an individual plays a role is partly determined by his unique psychodynamic make-up, which also determines the pattern of anxiety evoked by any given role. Different roles evoke different types and amounts of anxiety in particular individuals. Though a father may look and dress like a father, go out to work and sit at the head of the table, he may, in voice, in deference, and in demand, act like a son, using his wife for a mother and treating his children like siblings. Such a father may constantly ask for mothering from his wife (he may even call her "mother"), ask her to intercede and decide for him, and expect her to carry the major responsibilities of the family. The father behaves as he does because of his unfulfilled childhood needs and conflicts, which claw at him so strongly that he cannot resist them. Such a pattern of role fulfillment is considered pathological, both because the man's childish behavior prevents him from fulfilling his other needs as an adult male and because the other members are being deprived of basic satisfactions—the wife of a husband, and the children of a father.

Many students of family life describe psychodynamic organization in terms of a series of what they call "transactional processes," or sets of emotional gestures and responses. This emphasis draws attention to the pattern of action, and particularly interaction, in family life and describes the family in terms of this pattern of action. Ackerman (1958), who pioneered much of the work in this area, demonstrated, for example, that there is a reciprocity between the psychopathological conflicts of the family members and the way in which they interact, and that many of these conflicts can only be remedied by changing their interactional patterns.

The studies of Jackson and his associates (1958) have shown how a distorted familial communication disturbs the behavior of family members. One of their main contributions has been the identification of what they call the "double bind," which is a form of communication in which the parent simultaneously or alternatively both welcomes and rejects the child. This is illustrated by the case in which the mother says to the child, "Darling, don't you love your mother? Come give her a hug." Then, when the child comes to her, she becomes frightened of the intimacy and says, "Why are you always clinging? Why don't you ever leave me alone?" Naturally, this "double bind," which can take many forms, has the effect of producing conflicting definitions of the relationship and intense subjective distress.

Wynne and his associates (1958) have described what they term "pseudo-mutuality" in the families of schizophrenics. Pseudo-mutuality exists when the members of a family feel that their relationship to each other is more important than their individual needs. The relationship is so intensely important to them that they stress mutuality at the expense of differentiation. In healthy families the mutuality and reciprocity of roles is congruent with the growth and development of the relationship and its members. However, in the case of pseudo-mutuality, the role reciprocity is rigid and takes place at the expense of the real and changing needs of the relationship and its members. Pseudo-mutuality involves a characteristic dilemma: Any divergence of opinions or roles is perceived by the family as a disruption of their relationship, which must be avoided; but if such divergence is avoided, the relationship becomes artificial. The authors found that families in which there is an intense and enduring pseudo-mutuality will, if certain other factors are also present, develop acute schizophrenic episodes in some of their members.

Lidz and Cornelison (1956) have hypothesized that the ego weakness of the schizophrenic is related to his introjection of his parents' weaknesses (typified by the case in which the mother is dependent on the child for fulfillment), to his introjection of parental rejection during the process of early identification, and to the fact that in such families the child is forced to identify with parents whose images have been seriously tarnished by their devaluation of each other. They found that many families were split into two factions by an overt schism between the parents. In these families the parents constantly attacked and undercut each other, and their recriminations and threats to separate were far more frequent than their efforts at mutual support. In the circumstances the child could not use one parent as a love object or model for identification without antagonizing the other. In other families they found that harmony existed only because the psychopathology of the dominant parent was accepted or shared by the other. As a result, the family environment became badly distorted or skewed, with a consequent distortion in the personality development of the children.

It is difficult to describe the emotional structure of family life—somewhat like trying to capture a moving series of lights and shadows. It can be seen in the system of emotional roles, in the texture of the relationships between the members, in their capacity to solve emotional problems, and in their manner of doing so, in the climate of their emotions, in their communication, and in their sense and need of freedom, autonomy, individuality, and dependency. All of these facets, and others for which we have no words, are part of the structure and texture of emotional life in the family. Yet not all of them are relevant to distinctions between families. Since we sought the distinctions and their relationship to the personalities of family members, our task was somewhat simplified.

Our first ideas about the relevant dimensions of psychodynamic organization came from the pilot study of the nine families with emotionally healthy children. Together, the psychiatrist and sociologist spent a year talking to these families, following the pattern of their individual and family lives, and finding out how they lived and what was important to them. We learned that they varied considerably both in the levels of their emotional health and in the patterns of their emotional organization, and we made these differences the axes of our inquiry. Finally, we set out to develop a set of questions that might be applied to all of the families, to identify and describe their differences. Those questions bearing upon the social, organizational, and community relationships of the family are treated elsewhere in this book. Those that follow we considered relevant to emotional organization.

Essentially, the questions inquired into the family's functioning as a unit and the emotional relationships between the members. We were interested in the family's capacity to meet and solve emotional problems, its attitude toward the expression of affect, the patterns and content of its communication, the kind of emotional roles played by the family members (did they stick to traditional roles? was there scapegoating?), and the presence or absence of psychopathology, typically in the form of conflicts in the handling of rage, dependency, passivity, and sexuality.

The relationships between the members of the family were examined with respect to the warmth and affection toward each other, the pattern of dominance between husband and wife, what they liked about each other, and particularly the presence and nature of role projections—that is, the views each held of the other: as a good or a bad self, a masculine or feminine self, and so on.

With these categories in mind, we analyzed twenty of the families in the major study—the families of the ten healthiest and the ten most disturbed students. The interview protocols and psychological tests were carefully reviewed and evaluated in terms of these categories by the psychiatrist. The categories were then coded and cross-tabulated with the emotional health of the children. Each family was described in terms of how it functioned in each subarea of family functioning and family relationships.

Since the evaluations were made by the same psychiatrist who made the emotional health evaluations, and who by this time was also fully familiar with the families, there was probably both tautology in his reasoning and contamination between the evaluations and the emotional health ratings. The reader should be aware of this. However, the process was valuable in articulating a psychiatric description of families that seems to differentiate clearly the healthy and the disturbed.

Briefly, the categories were as follows: The categories of family functioning were the capacity to recognize and solve emotional problems; the amount and kind of communication; the degree and type of affective expression; the degree of autonomy permitted to family members; and the presence or absence of psychopathological problem areas in three or more members of the family —for example, problems in handling rage, dependency, passivity, or sex. The categories of family relationships were the degree of warmth and affection between individuals; the balance of dominance between the parents; and the kind and degree of role projection by the parents with respect to each other and the children. Actually, the categories were a bit more detailed; we have simplified them to avoid confusion.

Each category was coded, usually into three or four subcategories like high, medium, or low, and cross-tabulated with the emotional health of the children, and frequently with many of the other categories. For example, with respect to the degree to which it was able to meet and solve emotional problems, a family was categorized as positive if it recognized and took steps to deal with these problems, negative if it denied or evaded them, or intermediate. These ratings were then cross-tabulated with the emotional health of the children, who had been categorized as healthy, intermediate, or disturbed, to give us a nine-fold summary of all the relationships between the two variables.

In almost every case we found that the categories clearly differentiated healthy and sick children, so that, for example, families with a very low level of psychopathology tended to have healthy children, while those with many areas of psychopathology tended to have emotionally disturbed children. However, a detailed study of the results suggests that many of the categories we employed may not in fact be distinct from each other, for they showed a high degree of interrelationship and produced almost the same distributions when cross-tabulated with the emotional health of the children. Where this was the case, we assumed that they functioned as indicators of the same underlying variable. Two groups of reasonably similar, interrelated variables appeared. They were problem solution and communication, and autonomy.

FAMILY FUNCTIONING

Problem solution and communication describe the degree of communication in the family, the capacity of the family to see and solve emotional problems, the amount of free interaction among the members, the degree of reciprocal warmth between husband and wife, and the presence or absence of psychopathological problems in handling rage.

We are not referring here to the amount of talking or physical activity in the family, for some of the families of disturbed children had plenty of both, but rather to the extent to which family members talked about things that were emotionally important to them, the extent to which they recognized and attempted to cope with emotional problems (rather than denying or trying to evade them), and the degree of spontaneity in their relationships.

At one extreme were thirteen families that evaded or denied emotional problems and tended to restrict their communications to instrumental affairs. The relationships among the family members were for the most part rigid and formal, and the husband and wife unaffectionate and cold. Three or more of the family members had severe psychopathological conflicts in handling rage. In all of these families both the husband and wife were emotionally disturbed, and in nine of them all of the children were disturbed. At the other extreme were seven families that showed a definitely positive approach to the solution of emotional problems and demonstrated a high level of communication and interaction among the family members. The husband and wife were warm and affectionate, and there were only moderate problems in handling rage. In all of these families at least one parent and one child were emotionally healthy. Two families had one child who was emotionally disturbed.

This dimension of family life actually reflects a kind of consensus and cooperation in the family, along with an openness and sense of security in the parents. It seems to reflect, especially, the influence of the father, for the one parent-child variable that appeared as part of this dimension was the degree of the father's spontaneity with his children. All of the fathers in the "healthy," or problem-solving, families enjoyed a definitely spontaneous and warm relationship with their children, whereas only three of the thirteen fathers in the "sick" families did. The ten others were rigid and found it difficult to relate to their children as people. Because of this difference in the two groups, we suspect that this dimension is linked to the father's role and perhaps influenced decisively by his preferences and personality.

Examining the relationship between the capacity of the family for problem solving and the emotional health of children, we found that among the seven families who had a positive approach to problem solving, fourteen of the children were healthy and two were disturbed; whereas among the thirteen families with a negative approach, only six of the children were emotionally healthy and eighteen were disturbed.

All of the families with emotionally disturbed children seemed completely unaware of the children's disturbances, even though in some cases the symptoms were quite severe and in one case an outside agency had recommended psychiatric help. Some of these children displayed gross symptoms of effeminacy, depressive withdrawal, or very severe and relatively incapacitating psychosomatic symptoms. Yet these problems were never brought to the attention of the research team, nor did the families make any attempt to cope with them. In many cases it seemed clear that the problems of the children functioned to meet some need of the parents. In contrast, the families with predominantly healthy children seemed aware of even the smallest problems and often brought them to the attention of the research team. In fact the healthier the person and the family, the more they seemed to experience a kind of self-discovery during the interviews, and gain perspective on their own lives. They themselves often brought up or discovered problems in their personal or family life, and usually asked for help or moved to correct the problems by themselves. We hasten to add that the matter was not really as black and white as our description may suggest, for even those families with predominantly healthy children sometimes had disturbed children whose problems they did not recognize; their nonrecognition was more rare, however, and their denial less complete.

We do not know how it came about that some of these families were so open and efficient in communication and problem solution and others so limited and ineffective. The latter may well be simply a reflection or consequence of the emotional problems of the husband and wife. However, it is clear that healthy and disturbed families differ sharply in problem solution and communication. This dimension thus emerges as a critically important factor in emotional health.

Problem solution refers to the way in which the family deals with threats to the physical or emotional well-being of the family unit and its members. Such threats might include severe disturbance or unhappiness or incapacity to function in individual members, or a disruption of the ways in which members provided emotional support, appreciation, or condolence to each other. When the members of our families were conscious of and attempted to solve such problems in a way that was not damaging to individual members or the equilibrium of the family, we called it positive coping. When they failed to identify the problem at the expense of a member of the family or of the family as a whole, we called it negative coping.

The judgment as to what constituted a problem was made by the trained psychiatric observer. This was not a particularly difficult task because families that dealt with problems by negative coping tended to accumulate them, so that they were found, so to speak, awash in their own problems. Those families who coped positively tended to take immediate steps to deal with the problem as soon as it appeared or they became conscious of it, so that in general they had few problems.

The poorly coping families showed a variety of problems:

A son with emotional problems refused to continue his education, though he came from an upper-middle-class family; the mother recognized his problems, but the father insisted that they did not exist. So the family did nothing.

A boy manifested such strong symptoms of effeminacy in speech, gesture, and associations that his siblings commented. It was clear that the family was denying the existence of the symptoms.

A boy suffered from such severe psychosomatic symptoms that he was incapacitated from time to time. Physical examination revealed nothing. The physician suggested psychiatric care, but the family refused to accept the suggestion.

A wife had severe conflict over sex, shown in a strong aversion to sex relationships, the denial of sexual relations to her husband, and a series of gynecological complaints and operations. The husband was extremely frustrated, but they failed to talk or do anything about the problem.

A girl in her late teens had never had a date, showed strong symptoms of denial of sexuality and general withdrawal, some paranoid thinking, and overdependency on the mother. Yet the parents noticed nothing.

There was a more general way by which we could have identified these negatively coping families, though we did not use it as a criterion; it was the way in which they reacted to the research project. Clearly, most of the families felt somewhat uneasy about being studied, though often for very different reasons. However, it was one of our earliest findings that the more emotionally healthy the family, the more likely it was to participate in the project. Among the families of subjects who showed the most severe pathology, more than 60 per cent refused to participate in the project. In those cases in which we met the families, they showed strong signs of protecting themselves and great anxiety about the project. Furthermore, those negatively coping families that did participate seemed incapable of dealing with the crisis of our invasion of their lives; we had the sense that it was a definite threat to them. In contrast, the positively coping families often said that they had come into the project in hopes of obtaining help with some problems, and in fact many of them seemed to find the project helpful, though the research team consistently refused to intervene therapeutically.

Examples of positive coping were more difficult to find than those of negative coping, for in general the positively coping families were marked by the absence of crises or problems. To a large extent this was due to the sensitivity and tenderness that the members of the family felt toward each other. They immediately recognized disturbance or unhappiness in the others and tried to help. Often this meant helping the other articulate his difficulties, giving him the chance to talk about them, and then, if necessary, taking some action. Husbands and wives gave each other a chance to air gripes or fears, and offered consolation or support. Where they were not in the habit of verbal expression, they might take steps to protect and support the other, giving special consideration and open affection. Most of the "crises" tended to seem minor, for these families had a sense of their own ability to meet and solve problems. Action was taken so quickly that the immediate emotional disturbance had little chance to grow or ramify into a family disturbance. As a result, it was very difficult to find examples of the ways in which such families solved problems. Some of those we did encounter follow:

> After the birth of a daughter, a mother showed emotional disturbance, largely caused by the proximity of a deranged neighbor. The father immediately arranged for medical consultation, though there were clearly no physical symptoms, and gave her strong support.
>
> During the research project a father came to realize that he was isolating his family and had been doing so for twenty years. He immediately arranged to take them on vacation and to increase their social life together.
>
> Parents became conscious of the emotional difficulties being experienced by a daughter and asked the research team to recommend psychiatric assistance.

One family was an especially good example of a positively coping family. It had no recognizable instrumental problems and dealt in an active and straightforward fashion with its one major emotional problem. During adolescence one of the boys began to reject school and play hookey. The family first attempted to meet the problem by discussing it among themselves and then by sending the boy to an excellent boarding school, which they hoped would better serve his needs. This ameliorated his school problems but revealed the other problems, such as overrebelliousness and defiance, that lay beneath. The family then consulted a psychiatrist. This was an unusual step for a family with their socioeconomic background and indicated a marked willingness and capacity to cope with affective problems. The family was able to work effectively with the psychiatrist and was helped considerably. As a consequence, both the family as a unit and its individual members gained considerable maturity and increased effectiveness.

One is reminded of Koos's (1946) discovery that well-organized families who succeeded in solving problems actually had very few, for it was the insolubility of the difficulty that made it a crisis. On the other hand, he also found that poorly organized families failed to solve problems, and the more they failed, the more problems they seemed to meet. Koos was speaking about what we would call instrumental problems, such as unemployment or sickness, but his findings are parallel to our observations of the ways families met emotional problems. We did not find that there was any difference in the ways healthy and disturbed families met such instrumental problems, so we suspect that the capacity of the family to meet that kind of problem is indeed related to the adequacy of their social organization.

Since the discussion of emotional problems is clearly a stage in their solution, it is evident that communication and problem solution overlap. Communication refers primarily to the level of directness and openness of verbal emotional communication among family members. Basically, it concerns the degree to which the members of a family discuss their feelings about each other and family issues. If one member is angry at another, does he say so and does he say it to that person?

We evaluated the communication in the family along two dimensions: clear-masked and direct-displaced. A clear message is one in which the feelings are frankly expressed and undisguised;

a masked message, on the other hand, is one in which the feelings are disguised or hidden. If the feelings are aimed at the person concerned, we call them direct, but if at a substitute target or person, we call them displaced.

In the pilot study, we were able to identify patterns of communication and to rate each of the nine families on the degree of communication in each pattern. We found that those who communicated a great deal, and in what we called a collective pattern (when they were together as a group, say at the dinner table) had the healthiest children, whereas those who communicated less and not collectively tended to have disturbed children. These were very interesting results, but unfortunately we found that the identification of patterns of communication with any precision called for a prohibitive amount of time spent in interviewing the family on this subject alone.

In the major study, we attempted to replace this interviewing by a set of specific questions supplemented by some interviewing. But we were unable either to make an accurate assessment of the form of communication or measure it with precision. Therefore we were forced to rely on our judgment; thus our ratings were only approximate. Fortunately, however, many of the families could be rated clearly high or low in level of communication. We rated the degree of communication in each family as high if there was abundant open and direct communication between the members of the family, and low if there was little of it. Thus families who communicated a great deal but in a displaced or masked form were rated as low. As before, the judgments were those of the psychiatric observer.

FAMILY RELATIONSHIPS

Warmth and affection constitute a dimension of family life that describes what we have called the welfare emotions, including the general capacity for love and the expression of love, tenderness, and care. It also describes the extent to which the husband and wife are satisfied with each other—that is, the degree to which theirs is a positive relationship in which they are both able to satisfy their needs and to feel secure, loved, and respected.

It is interesting to note that where there is such a relationship, the partners seem to satisfy so many of each other's needs that they are, in a sense, sufficient unto themselves. Thus we found cases where the husband or the wife suffered from rather severe psychopathology, but the children were perfectly healthy. These were all cases in which the married couple had a warm, supportive relationship, which seemed to act as an insulator, protecting the children from the psychopathologies of the parents. When the parents do not satisfy each other's needs, they must turn to the children and impose on them in some way or other, often producing emotional pathology in the children.

Rage is angry, hostile arousal. It is considered adaptive if it helps the individual resolve the problems that inspired it, or reduces his intrapsychic tensions without hurting others. However, many are so disturbed by their own anger that their chances of adaptation are actually reduced and their difficulties aggravated. Out of fear and lack of control they resort to suppression, repression, denial, projection, or displacement.

Members of the Protestant middle class usually fear anger as evil and destructive. Therefore they usually feel guilty if they indulge in it. (This is particularly true of women, since rage is an emotion that, if accepted at all in our society, is considered appropriate only to men.) We found, indeed, almost no one who was free of conflict and many who experienced rather severe conflict.

If in a family three or more members suffered from psychopathological conflict in expressing and controlling rage, we characterized the family as having problems of rage.

The father's spontaneity with the children refers to the ease with which the father talks and interacts with his children. Can he express both tenderness and anger? Does he spend time with them? Can he see them as individuals and act toward them in ways that are appropriate to their age? Some fathers can relate to their wives but not to their children, and some relate to no one. Such fathers have a very strained or rigid relationship with their children. Should their children approach them with an emotional problem they simply would not know how to react. We rated such fathers as very low in the degree of spontaneity with their children.

This was the only parent-child variable that appeared as part of the problem solution-communication group. Its appearance suggests that this group of variables is strongly influenced by the role of the father in the family. When the father has a positive relationship with his wife and children, he can provide sufficient stability to family life to enable the members to talk and solve problems and accept and handle rage.

Tables 2 and 3 present the relationships of each of these variables to the emotional health of children and to problem solving.

In Table 2 each of the variables shows almost the same distribution to emotional health of the children. Table 3 indicates that each variable is closely related to problem solution. In fact the relationship is often so perfect that the variables cannot be distinguished. Together these two tables present the evidence on which we based our decision to group these variables together and refer to them collectively as one dimension.

Autonomy-dependency is another dimension that describes how the members of the family are related to each other. It refers to their dependence on each other and to the amount of autonomy that they permit and encourage in each other. Both dependency and autonomy are present in any close human relationship, but when the family insists on complete sharing and conformity, the dependency can be pathological and the autonomy almost nonexistent. Our findings suggest that it is the mother rather than the father who most influences the balance of autonomy-dependency. Her consistency in dealing with the children, her mode of discipline, whether directional or constrictive, her participation in their activities, and her spontaneity, or lack of it, in her relationships with them all seem to be part of the way in which autonomy and dependency are manifested in the daily life of the family.

Because we feel that the central issue is autonomy, and because its cross-tabulation with the emotional health of the children is almost exactly that of the other variables in this group, we have chosen it as a representative variable. It is, we think, a key variable in the emotional climate of family life. For one thing, the degree to which the mother and father can detach themselves from their own

Table 2

Problem Solution-Communication Variables and Emotional Health of Children

Degree of emotional health	Problem solution		Communication		Free interaction		Husband-Wife affection		Problems[a] in rage	
	High	Low	High	Low	High	Low	High	Low	High	Low
Healthy	14	6	15	5	15	5	14	6	4	6
Intermediate	2	4	3	3	4	2	2	4	3	3
Disturbed	5	15	5	16	8	13	2	19	3	18

Father's spontaneity with children

	High	Low
Healthy	15	5
Intermediate	4	2
Disturbed	8	13

Table 3

Problem Solution and Related Variables

Problem solution	Communication		Free interaction		Husband-Wife affection		Problems[a] in rage		Father's Spontaneity	
	High	Low	High	Low	High	Low	High	Low	High	Low
High	6	1	8	1	7	0	16	1	8	2
Low	2	11	1	11	0	13	1	12	0	10

[a] In the category "Problems in rage" we have reversed the tables so that High means the lack of such problems.

parents is crucial to their ability to function as mature adults and parents. It is a matter of the amount of autonomy they have achieved in their own development. If it is large, they are able to relate to each other as adults and mature men and women, and at the same time to take on the responsibilities of parenthood and permit their own children to develop autonomy. On the other hand, if they have not achieved much autonomy, there is a strong chance that their relationship with each other contains elements of infantile dependency, that they are not able to function well as parents, that they may compete with their own children, and that they probably do not permit their children autonomy.

Autonomy refers to the ability and freedom of family members to make their own choices and decisions, as well as to their sense of their separate identity. It also refers to family expectations about such freedom and individual responsible action. We attempted to evaluate the degree of autonomy in the family members by asking them how they made decisions, how the other members of the family reacted to their making certain decisions, and how dependent they were on others in such matters. When we felt that the family respected the right of, and in fact wanted, each member to make his own decisions, and when each member did actually make as many of his own decisions as possible, given his age and the interests of the other members of the family, we thought of the family as being autonomous. When, as in some families, the parents made all the decisions for the children, or action seemed to take place without decisions, or when the parents tended to be very dependent on each other or on their own parents, it was clear that the family suffered problems in autonomy.

We consider autonomy of great importance because it represents one of the key problems that the family has to solve. As is well known, the infant makes little distinction between itself and its mother, being deeply dependent on and identified with her. To a limited degree this attitude remains throughout childhood, since the parents remain deeply concerned with the child's welfare and behavior, and the child remains physically, emotionally, and socially dependent on them. Yet while we expect some of this dependence to continue throughout childhood, we also recognize that the child must develop his own sense of identity and gradually assume responsibility for his own actions. Both the school and the peer group lead and force him to act in ways different from his family's and to take responsibility for his own behavior. Indeed, if any individual, particularly a male, is to function in our society, he must make some progress in this direction.

The task is, however, a very difficult one, for the emotional ties binding the child to the parents are the strongest we know of, since the family is probably the main source of pleasure and security in the life of the child. If he gives up his dependency it may be with difficulty, and most people do indeed find it difficult to achieve independence and autonomy. The difficulty is aggravated by the love-orientation and love-withdrawal discipline measures emphasized in North American middle-class society. Yet difficult though it may be, unless the growing person can achieve a sizable measure of autonomy, he will never develop a satisfactory and firm ego identity. Furthermore, without some capacity for autonomy, the person will find parenthood difficult and may well pass on the same difficulties to his own children.

In the analysis of our families, we found autonomy linked primarily to such activity variables as the degree of activity and vitality in family life, the modes of discipline employed, the success with which the wife played and accepted her role, and the degree of the wife's spontaneity with the children. This seems to indicate that the internal life and actions of a family are strongly dependent on the wife-mother. Evidently, it is she who sets the standards for autonomy, acting autonomously herself and permitting and encouraging autonomy in her children. To some extent, this attitude by the mother seems to be a product of her emotional health, for we found that all mothers who were emotionally healthy had families with a high degree of autonomy. However, it is also clear that the autonomy is not a simple consequence of this emotional health, for a large proportion of the disturbed mothers also had families with a high degree of autonomy, though the disturbed mothers accounted for all the families without autonomy.

This fact is partly explained by our findings that the couples who showed reciprocal warmth and affection and free verbal and nonverbal interaction were also those in which the wife was rated high in the performance of her role and in spontaneity with the children. In other words, the ability of the husband to give his wife support, love, warmth, and contact seems to contribute to a satisfactory level of functioning on her part.

We now describe the subsidiary variables in the autonomy group. Each of these variables was evaluated in each of the families in the study.

Dependency refers to the unresolved dependency needs present in the relationships among family members. It is exemplified in the following cases:

> The father had retreated completely from the father role, taking an infantile role of dependency in relation to his wife. He functioned like a weak child in the family, obviously creating a distortion of the family patterns.
>
> The mother's dependency needs were manifested in her marked problem with obesity. She was a very dependent individual who resorted to fantasies of infantile and adolescent omnipotent gratification.

Obviously, where such problems are widespread in the family, autonomy is impossible. The behavior pattern and sense of liberty that characterize the autonomous family are impossible when its members have such seriously unresolved infantile dependency needs. Dependency is clearly the negative side of autonomy.

Affect and activity refer both to the ability of the family to act with appropriate affect and to its general tone of vitality, or liveliness. Families full of enterprise and enthusiasm for what they are doing can easily be distinguished from those who lead very restrictive, routinized, and emotionally flat lives. In families with a high degree of activity, one finds that most of the members are busy with many activities and that they express a great deal of appropriate emotion about these activities. There are, of course, families who are active but affectively flat, and these families have been classified as low in affect and activity. Families with a low de-

gree of activity seem withdrawn from life, restricting themselves to
what is necessary. Even among themselves there is little open expression of feeling.

The mode of discipline refers to the ends toward which discipline is directed: to keep the child from doing things, or to guide
him toward things that the parents want him to do. Naturally, no
mother uses only one form of discipline; even the most masterful
mother must sometimes use constrictive measures, for the baby who
tends to wander into the busy street must be restrained. However,
the mothers in our sample seemed to emphasize one mode or the
other. The difference is exemplified in the way in which parents
deal with their children's friendships: they can either keep their
children from what they regard as bad company by restricting their
circles of acquaintances and punishing them for stepping outside
them, or they can give them free rein and teach them to choose.
The differences seem to arise from the general orientation of the
mother, for whom the world can be either a fearful place from
which it is best to withdraw and protect oneself, or a way to satisfaction, a path on which one must learn to make the right choices.
These orientations are reflected in the various ways of dealing with
children. Basically, the distinction between directive and constrictive discipline lies in the extent to which the mother keeps the
child's needs in mind when applying the discipline. When, for example, she prevents the child from doing something for which he
is not ready and by which he may be harmed, her discipline is
directive. However, when discipline is primarily for the convenience
and in the interest—legitimate or otherwise—of the parents rather
than the child, it can be regarded as constrictive.

The mother's functioning in her role refers to the degree
to which the wife-mother performs the roles of homemaker and
mother efficiently and happily, and enjoys sexual relations and
functions relatively satisfactorily in that area. There is reason to
believe that her performance in her role is related to how much
she feels that what she is doing is a way of expressing love and
respect for the other members of her family. Also, on the deepest
level, it must certainly be affected by the meaning of the role to
her own needs. In other words, successful performance, as we have

judged it, implies more than mere superficial competence; it includes the idea that the mother takes pleasure in her tasks and sees them as part of the love that she feels for the other members of the family. It would also seem natural that the modes of discipline of such a mother would be directive rather than constrictive, and that her relationship to her children would be warm and spontaneous.

One must also assume that such a mother is relatively free of unresolved infantile dependency needs; otherwise, her performance of her tasks as homemaker, wife, and mother would be primarily in the service of fulfilling these pathological needs. With this kind of orientation, she herself would not be capable of autonomy, could not permit it in others, and would feel that she had to constrict her children. It would imply rigidities in the character structure antithetical to a warm and spontaneous relationship with her children or husband.

There were several mothers in the sample in whom the presence of dependency conflicts did not interfere with their successful role performance. This success seemed to be due to their good fortune in having strong, firm, but loving husbands. These men seemed to be able to give their wives sufficient love and support to satisfactorily assuage their infantile cravings and thereby prevent any of the expected negative effects.

The mother's spontaneity and warmth with the children is a category that is self-explanatory. Mothers who rated high on this variable had relaxed and positive relationships with their children, whereas those who rated low tended to be either tense and overstrict or remote from their children.

Tables 4 and 5 present the cross-tabulation of each of these variables, first with the emotional health of the children, and then with the autonomy variable.

It can be seen that each of these variables gives almost the identical distribution when cross-tabulated with the emotional health of the children, and that they are all highly correlated with autonomy. Together we feel that they reflect the activity tone of the family's life and the sense of respect that the family members have for each other's freedom, and for each other as individuals.

Table 4
AUTONOMY VARIABLES AND EMOTIONAL HEALTH OF CHILDREN

Degree of emotional health	Autonomy		Dependency		Activity		Discipline[a]		Wife's role[b]		Wife's relationships with children	
	High	Low	Low	High	High	Low	Const.	Dir.	Succ.	Uns.	Good	Bad
Healthy	18	2	18	2	18	2	19	1	18	2	19	1
Intermed.	3	3	3	3	3	3	3	3	5	1	3	3
Disturbed	9	12	5	16	9	12	7	14	8	13	7	14

Table 5
AUTONOMY AND RELATED VARIABLES

Autonomy	Dependency		Activity		Discipline[a]		Wife's role[b]		Wife's relationships with children	
	Low	High	High	Low	Dir.	Const.	Succ.	Uns.	Good	Bad
High	9	2	9	1	9	2	8	3	8	2
Low	1	8	1	9	1	8	2	7	2	8

[a] Dir. = Directive; Constr. = Constrictive.
[b] Succ. = Successful performance; Uns. = Unsuccessful performance.

82

Furthermore, the key to this activity tone seems to be the mother, for it is hers rather than the father's attitudes that are found most closely correlated with autonomy.

Each of the twenty families was carefully examined to determine the presence or absence of various kinds of psychopathology in each of the members. If both parents and at least one child displayed the same psychopathological conflict, the family was categorized as psychopathological in that area.

The number of different kinds of psychopathology was much higher in the families of the disturbed subjects than in those of the healthy subjects. All families suffered from some degree of psychopathological conflict in the handling of rage, evidently a product of our Western, Protestant restraint and need to contain the evil in man. However, these conflicts were much more marked among the families of the disturbed subjects, all of which had severe conflicts in this area. There were very few areas of psychopathology that marked all of the families of disturbed subjects. We could find only three: conflicts in the handling of rage, in unresolved infantile dependency needs, and in sexual functioning and identification. Since these three areas characterized almost all of the families of disturbed subjects, they might be regarded as the major dynamic problems faced by families from this socioeconomic setting. It is interesting that these are, in fact, the areas in which one might expect to find problems in such families. We have already commented on the reason for finding conflicts in the handling of rage. It seems equally plausible that these English Protestant middle-class families would pay the price of their pattern of inhibiting any overt expression of affect, and of their excessive rigidities in sexual training and education. This group seemed to reject the body and to prize puritanical definitions of sexual behavior. It is inevitable that exposure to such attitudes would lead to difficulties in sexual identification and functioning.

We were impressed by the widespread existence of affective deprivation among our subjects. This deprivation was aggravated by conflicts over unresolved dependency needs. It would be naive to believe that such conflicts were generated by a single factor rather than by a multiplicity of associated factors. However, we feel that the tendency of this group to value affective constriction and the inhibition of emotional expression in their interaction led to considerable affective deprivation in their interpersonal contacts, and the consequent production of unfulfilled dependency needs. Parents who have never developed the capacity to give warmth and affection are unable to supply their children with the necessary quota of this sustenance. Their failure leads to a chronic lack of fulfillment of infantile dependency needs. We feel that such families' use of love-oriented training techniques, which reject physical punishment in favor of giving love conditional upon acceptable performance, has the effect of tightening the bonds of dependency.

There were a number of other psychopathological areas that appeared in some, but not all, of the families of the disturbed subjects, and that were almost never present in the families of the healthy ones. These areas were passivity, withdrawal, depression, and difficulties in establishing close interpersonal relations. Since none of these characterized a majority of the disturbed families, we cannot regard them as a product of this way of life, nor can we really find an explanation of their etiology in our data. However, it seems clear that in particular cases these psychopathological conflicts in the parents present an important factor in the etiology of the problems of the children.

No definite conclusions concerning the etiology of psychopathology in the family can be drawn from our findings, for we only managed to catch these families at a moment in time, and our conclusions are, by the nature of the analysis, retrospective. Certainly, however, the psychopathology of the parents seems a tremendously important and, in some cases, determining factor. When both parents are emotionally disturbed it seems almost certain that their children will be disturbed; when both are healthy it seems equally certain that their children will be healthy. But even if one parent is disturbed, ordinarily at least one parent has some measure of emotional health, and this gives the children a way out. The problem then becomes: Under what conditions do they escape?

Before discussing this problem, we should note that our judgments concerning emotional health of the parents were made at a point in their careers when their marital experiences had substantially influenced the state of their emotional health. For example, in one of our families both parents had shown signs of depression and difficulties in sexual identification at the time of marriage. In the husband this was manifested in frequent migraine headaches and an almost total lack of dating or interest in women right through his college years. In the wife it showed up in developing signs of rejection of femininity, in the neglect of her appearance, and also in the lack of dating. Yet it was clear that the psychopathology of each had not aggravated the other's condition and that, in fact, they had welcomed the reciprocal timidity and withdrawal in the area of sex relations. With the passage of time, the man was remarkably successful in his career. He had come from an extremely poor laboring family and risen to a position of considerable eminence in Canadian industry. With these successes he became more secure, lost his migraine headaches, and began to function more aggressively in the area of sex. In turn, his increased security helped his wife, and his increased sexual attention built up her sense of femininity, and a positive reciprocal process was set into motion. At the time of the study, some twenty years after their marriage, they were both sexually active and emotionally healthy, and what is more, all of their children were healthy.

This example illustrates what we consider to be one of the most important findings concerning the psychodynamics of family life, and the factor most critical to the emotional health of the children—the relationship between the husband and wife. It is the character and structure of this relationship and what it means in terms of the self-concepts and satisfactions of the married couple that is critical to the emotional health of the children. Where the marital relationship is a warm and positive one in which there are mutual affection and respect, and in which each of the partners makes the other feel worthy and sure of his identity on all levels (sexually, as a member of the community, and as a parent), the relationship seems to absorb the psychopathologies of the parents, so that their children carry none of the burden. Where this is not the case—that is, where the partners do not respect or feel affection for each other, and where the husband and wife tend to erode the identity of the other—the parents almost always involve their children in their problems and in many cases trap them into serious psychopathology.

In the pilot study our most outstanding finding was this discovery that there seemed to be a direct relationship between the degree of emotional health found in the children and the degree to which the relationship between the parents was positive in the ways we have described. The success of the relationship seemed to rest on the attitude of the wife toward her husband. The most positive relationships were those in which the wife demonstrated what we called the "adoration pattern," in which she literally felt that her husband was the perfect man for her and had been responsible for most of the good things that had happened to her in life. Ordinarily, where this pattern existed the man seemed to play a relatively strong role in the family. Furthermore, where the woman felt this way, she remained deeply satisfied with her role as mother and housewife, and as we have pointed out earlier, this attitude is linked with her capacity to provide a form of organization in which the members of the family achieve considerable autonomy.

Thus there seem to be two ingredients in the "adoration pattern": the woman who needs a relatively strong man, and a man with such characteristics. We do not mean that the desired relationship is necessarily patriarchal, though this is a definite possibility. In many of the families where this relationship existed, the father seemed to play a relatively moderate role; most important decisions were only reached after considerable discussion between the parents. In one case the couple had almost no sex life, for the woman suffered deep fears and had never achieved anything more than extremely poor identification. Yet their relationship was so positive in other ways (including the fact that the woman did seem to appreciate her husband as a male, and he was extremely fond and protective of her) that they were extremely satisfied and happy, and their children were a pleasure to behold.

The husband-wife relationship seems to be the emotional thermostat of family life, reacting to the various forces that impinge on the family—forces like the personality needs of husband, wife, and children, crises, difficulties and satisfactions with the functioning of the family, and demands of the culture and the society. Just as the husband-wife relationship responds to these forces, so do the emotional climate of family life and the emotional health of family members respond to the character of the husband-wife relationship. While it is possible that some of these responses may be relatively rapid and short-term, most take place over a long period of time and should be seen as structural, or customary, aspects of the life of the family.

We have described two broad aspects of the psychodynamics of family life in terms of the capacity of the family for problem solving and communication, and in terms of the amount of autonomy permitted the family members. It is probable that these states actually consist of groups of more specific, potentially distinguishable states that would be more powerful predictors of emotional health. However, we have no confidence in our ability to evaluate or measure these with sufficient accuracy to warrant making generalizations about them. Our use of gross categories like problem solving and autonomy was the result of a deliberate decision to restrict our generalizations to the level of abstraction where we could write with confidence.

In summary, the families of emotionally healthy and disturbed children were distinguished by marked differences in their characteristic psychodynamic sets, and particularly, by differences in the areas of problem solution and autonomy. Problem solution was a name given to a complex of activities including the amount of emotional communication, the degree to which the father was warm and spontaneous in his relationships with his children, and the character of the husband-wife relationship. Because the father's relationship to the children was the only parent-child variable that appeared in the complex, we believe that the father is the critical person in the determination of the nature of the problem solution-communication process.

Autonomy was the name given to the other complex, which included the variables of problems in dependency, the amount of affect and activity, the nature of discipline, and the degree to which the mother's relationship with her children was warm and spontaneous. This complex seems to depend on the mother since it is closely related to many of her relationships and activities in the family.

Thus the two specific dynamic sets seem linked to the two major family roles: husband-father and wife-mother. It is our belief that these two sets represent the reactions of the marriage partners to their own relationship. When their relationship meets their needs satisfactorily, permitting and supporting their particular identities and sense of worth, each brings to the family a positive orientation in the psychodynamic set he influences, and the family is a durable and happy one with emotionally healthy children.

Of course, there are bound to be other factors influencing the character of the psychodynamic set. It seems very probable that in families in which there is a high degree of positive problem solving, the father is the kind of person who is accustomed to meeting and solving emotional problems in the course of his occupational life. Similarly, when the family has a high degree of autonomy, it seems likely that the mother is herself a person of considerable maturity, without severe unresolved dependency needs. In any case, the character of the husband-wife relationship seems to be an essential ingredient, for it can reinforce or weaken other predispositions, and itself goes a long way toward creating the conditions in question. Furthermore, the relationship is in itself of importance to the emotional health of the children, as a model of heterosexual relationships and a way of life.

Why are both problem solution and autonomy critical to the emotional health of the children? The positive solution of emotional problems seems to have two important functions in supporting emotional health: It helps build the healthy personality by dealing with emotional problems at their inception, thus preventing them from growing and ramifying; and it is, we believe, one of the factors establishing the problem solving capacity that characterizes the strong ego. The child who experiences a family strong in its solution of emotional problems grows into an adult who can solve his own problems.

Autonomy seems to be essential for the development of a satisfactory ego identity, for one must be permitted to consider oneself a separate person, and experience oneself as such, to find an identity. Without such autonomy it seems likely that the child would be unable to solve the basic problem of separation from his family of orientation and would remain overdependent. In our society this would seem to lead inevitably to some degree of emotional illness.

CHAPTER **5**

Social Class and Mobility

Though the families in this study belonged on the whole to the same social class, they exhibited great differences in degree and pattern of social mobility, and these differences proved important in explaining variations in their emotional health. We assumed that differences in social mobility affected the relationships between family members and the images that each had of himself and the others. Thus class and mobility were treated as part of the internal organization of the family.

We used Hollingshead's (1958) two-criteria index (occupation and education) to analyze intergenerational social mobility, and his three-criteria index (occupation, education, and place of residence) to identify social class. The effects of status and mobility were studied from four points of view: status difference, or the relative social status of the spouses at marriage; social class, measured in terms of the father's status; father's mobility, represented by the difference between the father's status score and that of his father; and mother's mobility, represented by the difference between the scores of the mother's husband and father.

It is said that the woman who marries up makes a good marriage, improving her lot in life and gaining the admiration of the community. Such a model of a "good" marriage also fits our cultural expectation that the male will be dominant and assertive, and the psychodynamic assumption that male assertion is linked to potency. On all these counts the woman who marries up makes a "good" marriage, whereas the one who marries down makes a "bad" marriage. We shall use the terms "good marriage" and "bad marriage" in this sense.

One can assume that emotionally healthy women will try to make good marriages* and that those who succeed will be rewarded by the approval of the community, the sense of success in life, and good relationships with their husbands. Conversely, one can assume that the woman who makes a bad marriage experiences strain and doubts about her own value as a person and completeness as a woman. In a cultural sense, she is degrading herself, which is always stressful. Since she is socially stronger than the man she marries, she may have the feeling that he is a weakling. A woman who becomes a housewife and mother commits herself to the framework of the family; a stressful marriage is a serious threat. This is not so true for a man since he has an alternative source of self-esteem in his job.

For the husband, a bad marriage may reflect dependency and weakness or exploitation. If either is the case, it adds another source of stress to the marriage. Yet a man usually marries for interpersonal rather than status reasons, choosing a woman for her charm and beauty rather than her status. A man makes a suc-

* Goode also reports that women who make good marriages tend to have higher IQ scores than those who make bad marriages.

cessful marriage when he marries a woman with attractive personal
qualities, a woman when she marries a successful man.

Table 6 examines the relationship between emotional health
and relative social status at the time of marriage.

Table 6
MARRIAGE UP OR DOWN AND EMOTIONAL HEALTH

Women

Degree of emotional health	Percentage Up	Percentage Down	N
Healthy	57	43	(19)
Intermediate	58	42	(19)
Disturbed	7	93	(13)

Men

Degree of emotional health	Percentage Up	Percentage Down	N
Healthy	40	60	(10)
Intermediate	53	47	(21)
Disturbed	70	30	(20)

The results show that most disturbed women marry down
and most disturbed men marry up. The emotionally healthy men
who married up and emotionally healthy women who married
down probably did so because of compensations like the emotional
health of their spouse. Our data show that all the four emotionally
healthy men who married up married emotionally healthy women,
whereas twelve of the fourteen disturbed men marrying up married
disturbed women. Among the women marrying down, five out of
nine healthy women and all the disturbed women married disturbed men. Thus the results show that our thesis holds only for
men.

We have suggested that men and women who make socially
successful marriages tend to have better relationships than those

who make socially unsuccessful ones. This was manifest in the sexual adjustment of the couples. We asked a small sample of couples, consisting of the parents of the ten most healthy and the ten least healthy of our subjects, about the frequency with which they had sexual intercourse. We were able to divide them into frequents, who had intercourse four or more times a month, and infrequents, who had intercourse less than twice a month. In all, we had reliable data on eighteen families. Since all of the couples had been married between twenty and thirty years, these represented relatively permanent patterns. Four of the six couples in which the woman had married up had sex relations frequently, whereas nine of the twelve couples in which the woman had married down had sex relations infrequently.

The size of our sample is too small to permit reasonable tests of significance. However, the direction of the relationship is quite clear. Two-thirds of couples who made good marriages had intercourse frequently, while 75 per cent of the couples who made bad marriages had intercourse infrequently. Though these results seem to confirm our hypothesis, they should be viewed with caution, for the emotional health of the wife is also predictive of the frequency of sexual intercourse, with five out of seven very disturbed women being infrequent, and five out of six healthy women being frequent. Since very disturbed women tend to marry down (93 per cent), there is obviously much room for confusion in interpretation.

Bad marriages seem to be related to the emotional illness of spouses and to poor marital relationships. Therefore they can be expected to cause emotional disturbance in the children. If the father is successful, his son should see himself as capable of success and find maleness a good and rewarding attribute—a firm step toward emotional health. But if father has been unsuccessful, his son may be uneasy in his maleness and experience considerable pressure from his mother, who wants him to succeed as compensation for his father's failure. The father may also press his son to succeed, both to relieve the pressure from his wife and to meet his own needs for success through identification. In this kind of family, maleness may well be regarded as bad, while at the same time the boy is required to succeed in the world of men. These are pressures conducive to emotional illness.

The daughter has a greater chance of escaping these parental pressures, for she is less liable to be used as the vehicle for the parents' unfulfilled ambitions. Our findings indicated that such is indeed the case. Status difference and the emotional health of boys showed a correlation of plus .391, which is significant at better than the .01 level of probability. There was no significant correlation between status difference and the emotional health of girls.

These correlations were based on the emotional health ratings of the original subjects. When we added their siblings to the sample and computed the percentages of healthy, intermediate, and disturbed in each of four status-difference categories, we found that the results confirmed our original conclusions. The relationship is shown in Table 7.

The results indicate that status difference does indeed influence the emotional health of boys but not girls. This seems to hold true even when parental emotional health is held constant.* We assume that this is because when the status of the father is higher than that of the mother, the father will have a status advantage within the family and the son will have a good role model and a greater chance of growing up in an integrated, happy family; when the status of the mother is higher than that of the father, she will feel dissatisfied, the family will be unhappy, and the father will be a bad role model.

Some further support for this explanation was found in the relationship between particular psychological characteristics of subjects and the difference in the status of their grandfathers. We found the following correlations between positive status difference (the father's status is higher than the mother's) and the personality scales of boys: MMPI—Hypomania, minus .406 (n-32); MMPI —Control, minus .300 (n-32); CPI—Responsibility, plus .414

---

* The sample was too small to permit a definitive test. But where the two independent variables (status difference and parental emotional health) might be expected to reinforce each other, they did. Thus among very disturbed women who married down, 77 per cent of their thirteen sons were emotionally disturbed, in contrast to 60 per cent of the sons of all women who had married down. Similarly, 50 per cent of the fourteen sons of emotionally healthy women who had married up were themselves healthy, in contrast to 42 per cent of the sons of all women who had married up.

Table 7

GRANDFATHER'S STATUS AND EMOTIONAL HEALTH

Paternal grandfather's status rel. to maternal grandfather's	Boys			
	Healthy	Inter-mediate	Disturbed	
		Percentage		N
Much higher	50	11	39	(18)
Slightly higher	27	20	53	(15)
Slightly lower	8	31	61	(23)
Much lower	0	29	71	(14)

Chi square 15.28　　.02　　Chi square not significant

Paternal grandfather's status rel. to maternal grandfather's	Girls			
	Healthy	Inter-mediate	Disturbed	
		Percentage		N
Much higher	30	10	60	(18)
Slightly higher	16	38	46	(13)
Slightly lower	31	15	54	(26)
Much lower	40	40	20	(5)

Chi square 15.28　　.02　　Chi square not significant

(n-32). All are significant at better than .05 level of probability. Each of these scales has some reference to tendencies toward productivity and self-control, with hypomania referring to tendencies toward marked overproductivity in thought and action, and responsibility reflecting maturity, self-control, and tolerance. Our correlations suggest that the greater the extent to which a man marries down and a woman up, the greater is the chance that their sons will not be hypomanic, will not have problems in control, and will be mature, self-controlled, and tolerant. On the other hand, the greater the extent to which the woman marries down, the greater is the chance that the sons will be overproductive and immature, with problems in self-control.

The families in this sample were almost all drawn from Hollingshead's Classes I, II, and III. There were only a few families from the lower classes, which is to be expected in a sample of the families of college students. The frequency distribution, by class, of the seventy-nine cooperating families was as follows: Class I, ten families; Class II, twenty-nine families; Class III, thirty-five families; Class IV, four families; and Class V, one family.

When the social class of the family and the emotional health of the children were cross-tabulated, a strong relationship was manifest between social class and the emotional health of boys, but not of girls. Table 8 shows the results of this cross-tabulation.

Table 8

HEALTHY AND DISTURBED BOYS IN THREE SOCIAL CLASSES

Degree of emotional health

Class	Percentage healthy	Percentage intermediate	Percentage disturbed	N
I	40	27	33	(15)
II	17	29	54	(35)
III	13	13	74	(32)

These differences in status do not have the same meaning for boys and girls. We think it is because in a class system the life expectations of the boy are delineated by the social class into which he is born. Since a man is measured by his position in the status system, the higher a boy's social class, the more secure he feels, the more he has access to power through correct background training, education, and social contacts, and the greater are his chances of obtaining the rewards of the society. The lower-class boy lacks these advantages, and experiences lessened self-respect and increased stress. He has to push himself harder and has less assurance of being regarded as a worthy human being.

For the girl, these stresses are tempered in two salient ways.

First, a woman is not deemed responsible for her success in the status system since she takes on the status of her husband. Second, and more important, in our society she is valued more in terms of her personal qualities than her achievements. This latter point applies primarily to the late teenager and young married woman; later in life a woman's worth is evaluated largely in terms of her husband's status. Then she may in fact react even more strongly than her husband to social status and mobility. In our culture, however, a young girl is given little intimation of these latter events, though her parents are, of course, deeply concerned with these later developments and thus with the social status and prospects of the boys she dates.

Our data confirm the hypothesis that the emotional health of college boys is definitely affected by their social class, whereas class seems unrelated to the emotional health of college girls. In later life there is a slight correlation between the emotional health of men and their social status and no correlation between the emotional health of women and the social status of their husbands.

In North America the successful man is one who rises to a job and position in the community better than those of his father, except of course where the status of his father is upper-middle class or higher, in which case he is successful if he reaches his father's status. Surpassing the father is upward social mobility. It has many interesting consequences for the man and his family. Since status and mobility have become standards by which the community measures the man and the man measures himself, self-respect is directly linked to them. On the psychodynamic level, since men gauge their manhood by the extent to which they match or surpass their fathers, those who do surpass them feel free and competent, and those who do not feel inadequate. Insofar as these are valid assumptions, we may say social mobility influences the development of the male personality.

The converse also seems to be true. In a competitive society where positions are allocated primarily on the basis of the qualifications of the candidate, personality plays an important part in success. The self-confident man who is not crippled by emotional blocks is better able to use his resources for success than is the anxious man who feels inadequate.

The matter is not so simple though. Other studies (Warner and Abegglen, 1955) have shown that many highly mobile men are emotionally disturbed, and what data we have suggest that this is correct. It seems that very high mobility can only be achieved at the cost of sacrifices in some other area of the man's life, such as heterosexual or family relations, and only men with pathologically imperious needs for success are willing to make these sacrifices. It should also be recognized that men who fail may actually be enacting a tragic fulfillment of neurotic needs for self-depreciation and effacement.

We believe that personality and mobility work together. Both a man's failure and his emotional disturbance present problems for the family. The fact that they tend to be conjoint may make these problems overwhelming. Perversely, similar overwhelming problems may emerge when a man is a great success.

We had both emotional health ratings and social mobility scores for fifty-eight of the fathers in our sample. Table 9 presents the cross-tabulation of these two variables.

Table 9

SOCIAL MOBILITY AND EMOTIONAL HEALTH OF MEN

Mobility[a]	Points	Healthy	Inter-mediate	Dis-turbed
Very high upward mobility	38 plus	0	3	4
Moderate upward mobility	19–38	6	12	7
No mobility	0–18	7	7	6
Downward (minus) mobility	minus 1–24	0	2	4

[a] The scale is based on seven points for change in occupational level (*e.g.,* unskilled to skilled worker) plus four points for a change in educational level (*e.g.,* some high school to completed high school).

It can be seen that the emotionally healthy men were neither very highly upwardly mobile nor downwardly mobile. Rather, they seemed to have done just about as well as their fathers, or slightly better. These findings support those of the Midtown Manhattan study (Srole et al., 1962), which showed a high positive association between social mobility and emotional health. They found that among men who were upwardly mobile there were one hundred who were healthy for every sixty-five who were disturbed; and that among the downwardly mobile there were 253 disturbed for every hundred who were healthy. The study did not report data on highly mobile men who were disturbed.

We found that men who had an upward mobility of 37 points or more (the equivalent of moving from mechanic to corporation president) tended to be emotionally disturbed. Actually, we had only nine men who were so mobile, but none of them was emotionally healthy and four of them were seriously disturbed. Generalizations cannot be made from such a minute sample, but we feel that this finding should be reported since it helps clarify one discrepancy that exists between the reports of other investigators. Whereas the Midtown Manhattan findings showed a positive relationship between upward mobility and emotional health, Warner and Abegglen (1955) found that big business leaders who had been highly mobile were characterized by such inability to form true intimate relations that they were lonely and isolated. We suggest that both extreme upward mobility and any kind of downward mobility lead to and reflect emotional pathology. In a society where mobility is such an important criterion of personal worth, it is to be expected that emotionally healthy men do, where possible, tend to be upwardly mobile. However, they do not seem willing to make the kind of major investment in time and energy necessary to great upward mobility since it ordinarily requires a sacrifice in satisfactions in the areas of a good marriage and parenthood.

It is difficult to say whether upward mobility is a cause or an effect of emotional health in men but, in the case of their children, if there is any relationship between the father's mobility and the children's emotional health, presumably it would be his mobility that affected their health. Presumably, upwardly mobile men would be good role models, provide for their families social honor, have positive views of themselves, and give their families the sense of being successful. Thus we expected that they would tend to have emotionally healthy sons.

Our findings did not support this theory, however, for we found a mild nonsignificant negative correlation between the fathers' mobility and the emotional health of their sons. We thought that this might be a result of the slightly negative relationship between very high mobility and the emotional health of the fathers, and indeed when we held the emotional health of the fathers constant, there seemed to be no relationship between the fathers' mobility and the emotional health of their sons, though it should be noted that the number of cases in each category was too small to permit accurate judgment. We also controlled by social class and found that only among Class III families was the fathers' mobility negatively related to the emotional health of the sons; among the Class I and Class II families there appeared to be a slight positive association. Our conclusion is that there is no association between the fathers' mobility and the emotional health of their sons, except insofar as mobility affects the emotional health of the fathers or the social status of their families, both of which are related to the emotional health of the sons.

The social mobility of the mother is defined as the difference between the social status of her husband and that of her father. If the status of her husband is lower than that of her father, she may feel deprived, no matter how successful her husband has been. Thus it is possible for a man to see himself as a success, while his wife regards him as a failure.

There seems to be considerable psychological stress involved in the housewife-mother roles. Possibly this is because the role is affective—that is, based on the mother's ability to give emotional support to her family—but imbedded in a rational, competitive society in which performance is judged by one's ability to meet impersonal standards set in nonaffective relationships. Only within an extended kinship system does the society support and reward the diffuse affective skills. Where the housewife-mother lives within an extended family or has many female relatives around her, or where the community is so small that there is considerable interaction among the women who appreciate the skills involved in the role, a jury of peers extends their admiration to her if she performs effectively. In our society, however, the affective orientation is thought to be appropriate only to inferiors—children and servants. The fact that many housewives report to researchers that they are "only" housewives demonstrates that they too accept this invidious definition of their role.

No one is satisfied to be a nonentity, and if the housewife-mother cannot depend on her competence in that role for self-esteem, she is forced, even more than her husband, to rely on the prestige derived from her status in the community. This is why some women seem more conscious of social status than men; it is the wife of the *nouveau riche* husband who is constantly on the make socially, rather than the man himself, for he can command prestige from the performance of his occupational role.

A woman who is downwardly mobile may feel, quite justifiably, degraded. Since her status and mobility depend on her husband's, she may blame him for this loss. The familiar pattern of recrimination in which the wife reminds her spouse of the fine prospects she turned down to marry him is brought to mind. The woman may blame all men and be angry with her sons as well as her husband. She may try to force her sons to compensate for their father's failure, or she may displace to the son the love for the husband she can no longer admire or respect.

All these tendencies—disrespect for the husband, hostility toward men, and displaced ambition and love—can be seen as pathological influences on the sons. Thus downwardly mobile women should theoretically have emotionally disturbed sons. As we noted in the case of status difference, the daughters probably do not experience the same difficulty. True, the stresses incident to this type of family are hardly conducive to emotional health, but they seem to weigh less heavily on girls than on boys. A mother is not as likely to direct so much hostility toward her daughters, though, if her hostility is directed inward so that she blames her femininity for her fate, she may well include them; nor is it as probable that she will displace either her ambitions or her eroticism to them.

We found a positive relationship between the mobility of the mothers and the emotional health of their sons. Among the sons of highly upwardly mobile mothers eight, or 53 per cent, were emotionally healthy, whereas this was true of only two, or 7 per cent, of the sons of downwardly mobile mothers. Among the latter group, seventeen, or 63 per cent, of the sons were emotionally disturbed. Table 10 presents these proportions in detail.

Table 10

SOCIAL MOBILITY OF MOTHERS AND EMOTIONAL
HEALTH OF SONS

Mobility of Mother

Emotional health of sons	*Percentages*				All boys
	High	Medium	Low	Downward	
Healthy	53	31	15	7	18
Intermediate	14	15	32	30	23
Disturbed	33	54	53	63	56
N	(15)	(13)	(19)	(27)	(84)[a]

[a] The total is larger than the sum of the column totals since it includes boys for whom we did not have data on the mother's mobility.

In interpreting these figures, the reader should keep in mind that in the whole sample 21 per cent of the boys were rated healthy and 56 per cent disturbed. Thus it is clear that the sons of mothers of medium and low mobility conform to the trends in the whole sample, whereas very upwardly mobile mothers have an inordinately high ratio of healthy sons and downwardly mobile mothers an inordinately high ratio of disturbed sons. The results strongly suggest that high upward mobility in the mother is conducive to emotional health in the sons, and downward mobility almost certainly conducive to emotional illness in them. These relationships persist even when the emotional health of the mother is held constant.

We have previously observed that the emotional health of the sons showed a mild negative association with the social mobility of the fathers. Since the reverse was true with respect to the social mobility of the mothers, we wondered what happened when the father was upwardly mobile and the mother downwardly mobile. Cross-tabulation shows that such families are destructive of the emotional health of the sons: Among the thirteen boys who had fathers who were upwardly very mobile and mothers who were downwardly mobile, 85 per cent were disturbed. This represents a higher ratio than the 63 per cent disturbed among the sons of all downwardly mobile mothers or the 78 per cent disturbed among the sons of all highly mobile fathers.

In summary, all aspects of class and mobility in the family are related to emotional health. The status characteristics of the family influence its internal organization, and this, in turn, affects the personalities of the members. The struggle to gain or maintain status affects the way that the members of the family feel about each other and themselves, and these feelings affect their interaction.

If the family's struggle for status has been successful, enabling its members to look with pride on their achievements and their position in the community, they tend to respect themselves and each other and to interact in ways indicating their approval and respect. In such an environment of mutual confidence, respect, and security, the weak personality is supported and sustained, and the strong personality thrives.

If the history of status shows failure, the wife feels that she has married down, both parents know that they have been downwardly mobile and the status of the family is low, the members find little on which to base respect for themselves or each other. The atmosphere may be one of mutual recrimination or withdrawal and the home a place of insecurity and anxiety. These conditions erode even a relatively strong personality and may destroy a weak one.

No family is ever independent of the community's standards and opinions, for not only does the community enforce them by bestowing or withholding power and privilege, but also the members of each family absorb them and judge themselves and each other accordingly. Since family relationships are probably the most durable and important of all relationships, these judgments powerfully influence the sense of self and the development and sustenance of personality. It is thus that the standards of the community become part of the web of family interaction, which is itself part of the personalities of its members.

CHAPTER **6**

Power and Authority

The power system of a family affects the personalities of its members in at least two ways: through its effect on the emotional climate of family life and through its effect on the superego and ego development of the children. The first effect is exemplified by Komarovsky's (1940)' finding that the legitimacy of the father's power was connected with the stability of family roles in crisis; by Herbst's (1954) finding that families with a balance of power (syncratic) showed the least tension; and by Blood and Wolfe's (1960) finding that wives in syncratic families reported the greatest amount of satisfaction in their marriages and in their husbands' love and affection. All these conditions are important to the emotional states of family members, and thus to their emotional health.

The effects of the family power system on the ego development of the children can be seen in numerous studies. Strodtbeck

105

(1958)', studying Jews and Italians in Boston, and Sangee (in Mc-
Clelland, 1958)', studying Japanese-Americans in Chicago, both
found the power of the father inversely related to the independence and initiative of the sons. King and Henry (1955) found that
mother dominance was related to depression in sons; Clausen and
Kohn (1960) found that it was related to schizophrenia; and
Bronfenbrenner (1961)' found that it led to dependency and irre-
sponsibility. Scott (1954)' discovered that both matriarchy and
patriarchy were related to a low level of adaptation in children.

Why is there a relationship between the power structure of
the family and the personalities of the children? We think that the
relationship exists because the personality, formed within a particular set of interpersonal relations, naturally reflects in its own organization the family patterns of work, power, and communication. When these patterns are congruent with the needs of the
family members, with the needs of the family as a social group,
and with the values of the larger society, they provide a strong and
efficient personality structure, which shores up, and even alleviates,
genetic or psychogenic pathologies. When the patterns are incon-
gruent or confused, they interfere with the functioning of the
family and leave the children with personalities that may aggravate
or give in to underlying pathologies. This is why some people with
relatively serious underlying psychopathologies function well, while
others with far fewer basic problems crumble in the face of adversity. It is true, of course, that certain psychopathologies find
therapy in adversity; but this is an explanation for another series
of events rather than a contradiction.

The distribution of power in the family is a key element
in family organization. The character, clarity, and legitimacy of
power distribution constitute an essential part of the family's role
relationships and functional efficiency. Both are likely to affect the
personalities of the children. Superego controls are introjected parental attitudes, and ego is at least partially constituted by the internalization of the family's modes of problem solution. If parental
attitudes, as manifest in decision making and discipline, are con-
tradictory, inconsistent, or destructive, one would expect to find
parallel states in the superegos of their children. Also, families who

are in conflict or without clear and legitimate power systems find it difficult to meet the recurrent problems of daily life and sometimes respond with denial or evasion. Children from these families do not know how to solve their own problems and have little confidence in their ability to do so—a manifestation of weak ego development.

Most families no longer accept the traditional sanctions for paternal dominance. As Homans (1950) has pointed out, its most obvious function, arising from the need for a business and military leader, has disappeared. Furthermore, as Bott (1957) discovered, when mobility uproots the family from the community, it also cuts it off from the traditional proprieties of maleness and femaleness. The suspicion, in the West, of any form of authoritarianism, and the changes in the structure of society and the approved models of character (Riesman et al., 1956; Miller and Swanson, 1958) provide other reasons. As a consequence, modern couples are afraid of authority, confused about what is "right," and prone to accept compromises like the democratic family council. Whereas in the community democratic organization is representative, with elected officials making all but the most important policy decisions, in the family it is often taken to mean equal power for every member and responsibility for none. This is no more or less than the evasion of responsibility, and families who make this choice often pay in indecision and structural chaos.

The weakness of community standards in our society gives psychological needs an unusual degree of influence in the power structure adopted in modern families. Thus, although democracy appears to be the standard, there are few sanctions supporting it; and where the psychological needs of the couple are strong, they may choose matriarchal or patriarchal forms.

A compromise between the alternatives of democracy and authoritarianism is father dominance or leadership. Because there lingers in our society a nostalgia for male leadership, which gives the father the lead without loss of self-respect, this pattern is feasible. Father-led families usually enjoy a high degree of democracy, but with the understanding, based on respect or tradition, that when necessary the father makes final decisions and settles conflicts.

The power system in the families in our sample was judged on the basis of eleven questions dealing with discipline, conflict resolution, decision making, and the members' impressions of which parent dominated.* Our system of scoring permitted us to score each question for the father, or the mother, or both. Using the cumulative scores from the eleven questions, we were able to determine the proportions of power of the husband and wife. We used these proportions to establish types of balance of power in the family. The questionnaire on which we based the authority scale was that of the student subject. His questionnaire showed the highest agreement with those of the other members of the family, and interviews confirmed that it was the most reliable and valid.

If the father received more than 65 per cent of the total score, we called the family father-dominant. If he received between 56 and 65 per cent of the score, we called it father-led. If the scores were relatively equal, so that the father received no less than 45 per cent and not more than 55 per cent of the score, we called it equalitarian. If the mother received more than 55 per cent we called it mother-dominant. Of the fifty-nine families in our sample, the largest part—nineteen families, or 33 per cent— were equalitarian. The others were: father-dominant, fifteen families, or 25 per cent; father-led, sixteen families, or 27 per cent; and mother-dominant, nine families, or 15 per cent.

A cross-tabulation of the type of power structure in the family with the emotional health of husband and wife is shown in Table 11.

As can be seen, the father-dominant form of family organi-

* The questions were developed in Bruck's (1963) comparative study of autocratic and democratic families. Bruck identified the authority patterns in the family through the use of extensive term papers written by the students and interviews with the students and their mothers about the patterns of authority in the family. Since she also asked her families (which were quite distinct from those in the Human Development Study) to fill out our Human Development Questionnaire, we were in a position to test and refine our scale with the help of her information. From a larger group we chose eleven questions that showed the highest power of discrimination between the different patterns of authority. Each was weighted according to its power of discrimination. When Bruck's twenty-four families were arranged according to the scores they received on our scale, all her democratic families fell into one part of the continuum and her autocratic families into the other.

Table 11

POWER STRUCTURE AND EMOTIONAL HEALTH
OF HUSBAND AND WIFE

	Husband		Wife	
Type of family	Healthy	Disturbed	Healthy	Disturbed
Father-dominant	0	10	4	6
Father-led	5	8	4	7
Equalitarian	4	11	6	9
Mother-dominant	0	6	1	5

zation attracts or creates only emotionally disturbed husbands, and the mother-dominant form both disturbed husbands and wives. There is little difference, as far as the emotional health of husband and wife is concerned, between the father-dominant and equalitarian family.

We assumed that in the English, Protestant, middle-class society from which these families were drawn, the norm would be father dominance or equalitarianism. These would be the approved forms, so that even when the wife says that it is the man who should "wear the pants" in the family, she still expects to have her say, and in many things to get her way. In fact, this may be true of all except some immigrant families; a study of fifty Montreal English working-class families showed that most couples believed that family decisions should be made together by the husband and wife (Crawford, 1962)'. Under these circumstances, one can expect that the men and women who follow this pattern receive considerable ego support.

But the matter goes deeper. If we consider the psychodynamic relationship between the husband and wife, it is apparent that we must think of both their sexual needs and their needs for mutual support and respect. Some degree of male domination appears necessary to the sexual needs for male assertion and female receptivity. In these terms we would suppose that either the father-led or the father-dominant family would provide a healthy environment. However, when we consider the needs for respect and support, it seems possible that the father-dominant family may be destructive. This leaves the father-led family as the ideal model, and this is in fact what our findings suggest. Since the emotional health of these parents was probably set before maturity, it was undoubtedly a strong force in determining the way they allocated power after marriage. Still, the data show that their emotional health was not the only determinant of the balance of power, and it is probable that once established, the power structure itself affected their emotional health.

We have already suggested that the balance of power affects the personality and emotional health of the children through its influence on superego and ego development and the emotional climate of the family. Specifically, equalitarian families tend to be confused, irresponsible, and characterized by an inability to resolve problems and a low level of sex differentiation, which creates difficulties in identity and ego development. Father-dominant and mother-dominant families involve an unacceptable use of power, which produces a tension-ridden, unstable organization; they are pathological in the poverty of the relationships between the parents, in the harshness and ambiguity of their attitudes toward the children, and in their failure to provide acceptable sex-role models. Further, these choices are not approved in our society—a fact that in itself exerts an influence on personality development.

The father-led family, which, according to our findings, is the only type producing predominantly healthy children, seems to provide the best synthesis. There is enough difference in the authority of the parents to differentiate sex roles, but enough sharing to maintain a positive relationship between the parents. The father is not harsh, the pattern is accepted in our society, and sufficient authority is centered in the hands of one person to keep the life of the family ordered and free of conflict. Children in such families have the advantage of well-developed and positive superegos, firm sexual identity, and strong egos. Table 12 presents a cross-tabulation of the emotional health of the children with the balance of power in the family.

Table 12 shows that both father-dominant and equalitarian

Table 12

POWER STRUCTURE AND EMOTIONAL HEALTH OF CHILDREN

Type of family	Emotional health of children			
	Percentage healthy	Percentage intermediate	Percentage disturbed	N
Father-dominant	29	13	58	(24)
Father-led	46	20	34	(35)
Equalitarian	17	19	64	(42)
Mother-dominant	7	53	40	(15)

Note.—The boys and girls were tabulated separately, but there was little difference in the ways in which their emotional health related to family power structures.

Chi squares show that the difference between father-led and father-dominant is not statistically significant, but that there is a significant difference between father-dominant and equalitarian families (chi square 7.55, which is significant at better than the .05 level) and between father-dominant and mother-dominant families (chi square 9.09, which is significant at better than the .02 level).

families produce far more disturbed children than do father-led families, and that mother-dominant families produce far fewer well children than do father-led families. Since the emotional health of the children is related to the emotional health of the parents, particularly to that of the mother, and since the parents' emotional health is related to the power structure, we thought that the emotional health of the parents might account for our findings. However, when we held the emotional health of first the mother and then the father constant, the relationship still persisted, though, as one might expect, it was much weaker.

There remains the problem of determining how the various distributions of power in the family affect the personalities of the children. Our information is based on paper-and-pencil tests administered to the student subjects. Each subject was given a battery of thirty-eight tests drawn from the California Psychological Inventory, the Minnesota Multiphasic Personality Inventory, the Guilford-Zimmerman Temperament Survey, and the Vassar College Attitude Inventory. We divided the range of scores in each test into high, medium, and low and made a frequency count of the number of subjects from each type of family who scored in each category. Since for most of these tests only the scores in the extremes have any meaning, we based our judgments on the difference in the number of subjects scoring high and the number scoring low. Thus we found that on the Guilford-Zimmerman Ascendance Scale seven children from father-dominant families scored low and one high, whereas seven children from father-led families scored high and one low. We interpreted this to mean that children from father-dominant families tended to be weak or have problems in the area of ascendance, while those from father-led families were strong in this area. Table 13 presents the frequency distribution.

The results from these tests revealed that most of the children from father-dominant and mother-dominant families had problems in many areas and strengths in few, whereas the children from father-led and equalitarian families showed no problems and definite strengths. However, in the first two cases the problems were different, and in the second two the strengths were different.

Father-dominant families tended to have problems in ascendance (G-Z: A), social maturity (Vassar: SM), and in the capacity for status (CPI: Cs). They showed strength only in the area of socialization (CPI: So).

Mother-dominant families tended to have children who were weak in ascendance, restraint, emotional stability, objectivity, thoughtfulness (G-Z: A, R, E, O, T), self-control, socialization, and flexibility (CPI: Sc, So, Fx), and who, according to the MMPI (D, Mf, Sc), showed symptoms of depression, sexual conflicts, and schizophrenia. They showed no areas of strength.

Father-led families tended to have children who were strong in ascendance (G-Z: A) and in emotional stability (G-Z: E). They showed no areas of weakness.

Equalitarian families tended to have children who were strong in restraint (G-Z: R), responsibility, tolerance, and sense of well-being (CPI: R, T, W), and who have no problems in Control (MMPI: C). They showed no areas of weakness.

To summarize, father-dominant families tend to have children who are timid, withdrawn, submissive, and without self-confidence, but who are at the same time compulsive, self-disciplined,

Table 13

SCORES OF STUDENTS ON PERSONALITY TESTS AND FAMILY POWER STRUCTURES

Test score:[b]	Type of Family[a]											
	Fa.-dom.			Fa.-led			Equal.			Mo.-dom.		
	H	M	L	H	M	L	H	M	L	H	M	L
Vassar Personality Inventory												
Vassar 113 Dominance; Confidence	0	5	5	9	2	3	7	5	4	1	4	4
Vassar 114 Social Maturity	0	5	5	4	6	4	7	5	4	5	2	2
Minnesota Multiphasic Inventory												
MMPI 78 Depression	4	3	3	3	6	5	4	5	7	6	3	0
MMPI 81 Masculinity-Femininity	2	3	5	3	5	6	5	7	4	6	2	1
MMPI 84 Schizophrenia	3	5	2	4	5	5	4	8	4	6	2	1
MMPI 88 Control	5	2	3	4	4	6	1	7	8	3	6	0
Guilford-Zimmerman Inventory												
G-Z 92 Ascendance	1	4	7	7	7	1	6	6	5	2	2	5
G-Z 91 Restraint	3	6	3	5	5	5	7	8	2	0	4	5
G-Z 93 Emotional Stability	2	6	4	7	6	2	6	7	4	0	3	6
G-Z 94 Objectivity	4	3	5	5	5	5	8	5	4	1	3	5
G-Z 96 Thoughtfulness	3	6	3	6	5	4	7	6	4	1	3	5
California Personality Inventory												
95 Responsibility	2	4	4	4	7	3	8	7	1	3	2	4
100 Tolerance	3	3	4	3	6	5	8	6	2	3	2	4
102 Self-control	2	4	3	5	4	5	5	8	3	1	3	5
105 Well-being	5	2	3	4	5	5	6	9	1	3	1	5
107 Socialization	7	1	2	1	11	2	7	3	6	1	3	5
110 Flexibility	2	2	6	2	8	4	6	3	7	6	2	1
106 Capacity for Status	1	2	7	5	4	5	7	6	3	3	3	2

[a] Fa.-dom. = Father-dominant; Fa.-led = Father-led; Equal. = Equalitarian; Mo.-dom. = Mother-dominant.
[b] H = High; M = Medium; L = Low.

113

and industrious. The children from mother-dominant families are just as timid and withdrawn but they lack self-discipline and industry and show serious psychopathological symptoms. In contrast, the children from both equalitarian and father-led families are better off. The children from equalitarian families tend to be quiet, friendly, and industrious—probably good followers and members—and the children from father-led families, more assertive and stable—probably good leaders.

The results largely confirm the clinical findings. Together they show that only the father-led type of family produces predominantly emotionally healthy children as determined by these tests and our evaluations. The mother-dominant type emerges as the most serious pathological type. The children from mother-dominant families face great difficulties in finding their own identity and individuality. The father-dominant family permits individualism, but almost at the expense of closeness and warmth. Besides, it is a less acceptable form in our society and perhaps for that reason more unstable. Both father- and mother-dominant families are poor environments for the rearing of emotionally healthy children.

It has often been assumed that there is some kind of a negative relationship between power and work, so that the laborer is subordinate. In fact this assumption is the basis of militant proclamations about the exploitation of the housewife and the need for reforms in family patterns. This controversy is not likely to be settled by logic, of course. But we felt that a little information might lend piquancy to the arguments; so we decided to cross-tabulate the patterns of power in the family with the patterns of work. Table 14 shows the results.

There is little relationship between power and work in the family. Clearly, most couples share the bulk of the tasks and divide the rest. We found no differences in the ways in which those with different patterns of power divided their work. Curiously, the few dominant mothers in our sample chose to do most of the work (probably because they were more competent), and the dominant fathers helped a great deal.

We have examined only one dimension of family organization, the pattern of authority. We determined that, of the patterns

Table 14
POWER STRUCTURE AND DIVISION OF LABOR

Division of labor[a]

Power structure	Balanced	Sharing	Traditional	Reversed
Father-dominant	7	4	3	0
Father-led	9	6	0	0
Equalitarian	8	5	2	2
Mother-dominant	0	0	2	0

[a] These patterns of division of labor are based on scores registering the relative participation of husband and wife in thirty-seven household tasks. The balanced family is one in which the father takes joint responsibility for at least 18 per cent of the tasks and shares at least another 15 per cent with his wife; the sharing family is one in which the father's participation is almost entirely on the sharing level; the traditional family is one in which the father participates in almost no tasks; and the reversed family one in which the father does more housework than the mother.

of authority chosen by our families, the father-led pattern best conformed to emotional health, was most efficient in maintaining order, and was considered most legitimate. But—and this is very important—this pattern of authority can be considered optimal only for the group from which our sample was drawn. This is a necessary reservation since all of the three general demands probably vary with the sociocultural milieu of the family. Thus differences in the sociocultural backgrounds of the parents may well give rise to different psychodynamic needs, the composition of the family (in terms of extension) may affect the efficiency of different patterns of organization, and different social classes and cultures may well result in different standards and expectations. In the case of any of these differences, we would naturally expect to find a difference in the optimal type of family organization.

CHAPTER **7**

Division of Labor

Work is one of the most durable aspects of the human condition. Most men work and find in their work a livelihood, a social status, an identity, and the key to their social relationships. Sociologists have long been aware of these allied functions and have studied work from many points of view. However, one kind of work, though universal, has been neglected. This is housework. As part of men's emotional lives, their feelings of security and well-being, and the formation of the personalities, it may well be the most important of all.

Housework, involving cooking, cleaning, maintenance, and the care of children, is essential to the everyday life of the family. By defining role similarities and differences, it contributes to identity and self-esteem, which affect the image that children have of their parents, and husbands and wives of each other; thus it affects the whole structure of the family's social and emotional relationships. Housework, too, more than any other kind of work, is an expression of care. Riezler (1950) maintained that it was only through care that human beings could show love for each other, and that work was the instrument of care. Care is essentially work done in the interests of another: For example, a woman who is cooking for a man with his health and preferences in mind is caring for him and indicating her love through her work.

For work to assume the meaning of care, the worker must see the relationship between his actions and some attitude he is expressing; otherwise, it becomes drudgery. The woman who likes to cook because she enjoys the satisfaction it affords her husband and children has joined work and care. Through her work she is expressing her love; and the work is in this way fulfilling.

When housework is seen as drudgery the interpersonal relationships in the family are affected. If the drudge is efficient, she implies self-sacrifice, making a kind of accusation that her mate desires to destroy her. If she neglects the housework, she suggests that the needs of the family are not of sufficient importance to her to make it worthwhile. The efficient drudge says "You don't care for me," the lazy one, "I don't care for you," and this communication is always understood within the family. To understand the effects of a mother's working outside the home, we can look at her view of housework. If her attitude toward housework, or some important part of it, remains positive, she can continue to give her family care. If she performs the housework grudgingly, or insists that someone else do it, she communicates her lack of concern for her family.

The father, too, must have a vehicle for care, and thereby a way to express his love. His occupation usually serves this purpose, though it can be solely an expression of his own interests or a means of escaping his family. The same considerations of attitude apply for him as for his wife. Most men also have some household responsibilities, which supplement their vocational expression of care.

The husband and wife need separate household responsibilities for many reasons. First, when there is no work because others do it, or no work to call one's own because it is all shared, people are robbed of the means of demonstrating love. The members of such families face serious problems in maintaining their relationships and communicating respect and affection for each other, as exemplified in the families of the idle rich for whom life is often meaningless, and the relationship between husband and wife so emotionless, remote, and formal that they must seek compassion elsewhere. Second, just as in the larger society, specialization of tasks in the household is essential to efficient functioning, for what is everyone's responsibility belongs to no one and is not likely to get done. Third, work structures interactions, and interactions form and support sentiments. The relationship of people is implicit in the relationship of tasks. As well as defining roles, the performance of reciprocal responsibilities gives a couple a sense of building together. Finally, a division of labor delineates personal and sexual identity. Man is not biologically endowed with the proprieties of sexual identity, but learns them from his culture. All cultures lay down rules of behavior appropriate to each sex and usually see different social roles as appropriate to each. Since certain tasks are culturally related to sex difference and the role-playing vital to it, work roles in the family support the development of identity. A father can participate with his son in sports at the same time demonstrating the appropriate behavior of the male in social interaction. He is also expected to be the man in the life of his daughter. The mother has reciprocal responsibilities. Each parent's fulfillment of these roles is remarked by the other, and this contributes to their feeling of communal effort and mutual respect. When their role differentiation is clear and appropriate to the cultural model, the partners are more certain of their sexual identities and more attracted to each other for these complementary qualities. Bott's (1957) finding that mobile couples who share rather than divide the work tend to be confused about sex roles lends support to this thesis.

The sharing of some tasks, which provides the solidarity of common experience, completes the picture of the ideal arrangement of family work. Apart from such obvious jobs as washing and drying the dishes, the care of the children is the prime area for satisfying this need.

A happy blend of the division and sharing of work seems to be essential to successful family life in our culture. Such a combination furnishes the means of communicating affection, accomplishing the necessary tasks, promoting respect, providing the satisfactions of a good job well done, and demonstrating appropriate role models for the children.

Our data on the division of labor in the family were based on the use of a modified version of the questionnaires used by Herbst (1954) in his Australian study. In our questionnaire we asked whether the father or the mother did each of thirty-three tasks often, sometimes, or never. The questionnaire was administered to each member of the family, and the results were compared. We found the highest agreement between the mother and father, but finally decided to accept the mothers' returns because these proved to be the most valid when checked against other data. We also asked the mother and father to fill out a similar questionnaire for their families of orientation, so that we would have data for the grandparental generation. These data, of course, suffer inevitably from forgetfulness, but they were our only clues.

The responses to the questionnaire were scored 3 for often, 1 for sometimes, and 0 for never. If the family indicated that the wife did the dishes often and the husband sometimes, she received a score of 3 on this item, he a score of 1. We computed the average score for the men and for the women for each of the thirty-three tasks. On the basis of the relative size of the average scores for men and women and the nature of each task, the tasks were grouped into four areas: men's work, women's work, common household tasks, and child care. Table 15 describes the average participation of the fathers and mothers in each task.

Two other sets of scores were subsequently computed from these data. The first were the total participation scores for the father and mother in each task area and all task areas together. If, for example, a father received a score of 12 in men's work, it might indicate that he had performed four of the six tasks often, or three often and three sometimes. This provided us with a measure of the relative participation of a particular husband compared to other parents in the sample; also, when compared with the wife's score,

Table 15
Participation in Household Tasks

	Father	Mother		Father	Mother
Husband's work			*Common tasks*		
Washes car	2.0	.3	Washes and dries all dishes	1.1	2.7
Mows lawn	1.4	.3	Washes dinner dishes	1.4	2.3
Shovels walk	1.6	.5	Carries groceries	1.1	2.4
Washes windows (outside)	1.3	.5	Empties garbage	1.6	1.6
Serves drinks	1.9	1.0	Gardens	1.4	1.4
Makes repairs	2.0	1.1			
Wife's work			*Child care*		
Plans meals	.2	3.0	Cares for sick child	1.1	2.9
Cooks meals	.6	3.0	Bathes child	1.1	2.9
Cleans house	.4	2.5	Puts child to bed	1.3	2.9
Makes beds	.5	2.6	Feeds child	.9	2.8
Writes thank-you notes	.6	2.7	Gets up to feed child	.7	2.8
Makes lunches	.3	2.3	Gets up if child cries	1.1	2.5
Washes windows (inside)	.5	1.8	Teaches table manners	1.9	2.7
Feeds and cares for pets	.8	2.0	Reads or tells stories	1.5	2.5
Buys groceries	1.0	2.9	Gets child up	1.7	2.4
Cooks breakfast	1.1	2.7	Helps with homework	1.4	1.8
			Participates in hobbies	1.4	1.3
			Participates in sports	1.5	1.1

120

it provided a measure of the division of labor in the family. The second set of scores showed for each family the proportions of the total tasks performed by the husband, by the wife, and by both together. With these proportions we were able to categorize families as primarily sharing, balanced, or autonomous.

Table 15 shows that each of the household tasks on our questionnaire was performed by some husband in our sample. Where the average score is 1 or less, most of the husbands (or wives) participated in the task only sometimes. Where the score is more than 1 and approaching 2, it can be assumed that this was a task often performed by a particular spouse.

As might be expected, very few tasks were the major responsibility of the husband. The average male participation in tasks labeled as men's work is 1.3 or better, and generally this is twice as great as the average female participation. Men also participate very much in the care of the children, which is thus a major area of sharing between husband and wife.

We used the mothers' and fathers' reports on the division of labor in their families of origin to compute participation scores for the grandparents. When we compared the two generations with respect to the proportion of fathers who participated in each of twenty household tasks, we found that fathers in the present generation participate more than three times as much in the washing and drying of dishes and almost twice as much in several areas of child care. We can assume, however, that there is probably poor recall concerning child care in the grandparents' generation and therefore that the finding of a change here is less reliable. Other investigators, however, have reported similar findings, which to some extent compensate for the poor reliability of ours.

More interesting than the reports of change are those of stability. In a period of great change in the family and in the roles of men and women in our society, it is interesting to find so little in the division of labor. In nine out of twenty tasks on which we can report, there has been no appreciable change between these two generations of parents, and the role of the women is substantially the same. The durability of these patterns, even in extreme situations, such as that of Russia, where, as Mace (1961) reports,

Table 16

DIVISION OF LABOR IN TWO GENERATIONS

Task	Grandfather's participation Percentage	Father's participation Percentage
Washed dishes	7	20
Made beds	1	10
Cleaned house	4	7
Planned meals	1	0
Bought groceries	13	13
Carried groceries home	21	21
Cooked meals	1	4
Carried out garbage	49	47
Washed windows	21	22
Bathed child	8	21
Fed child	10	12
Put child to bed	17	25
Read to child	31	30
Helped child with homework	19	26
Taught table manners	41	52
Took care of sick child	18	15
Engaged in sports with child	23	40
Got up with child during night	23	20

Russian women continue to do most of the housework even though they all have full-time jobs, suggests that this pattern of work has unanticipated functions: that is, it allows for care, reinforces sexual identity, and provides role models for the children.

FAMILY TYPES

We categorized our families according to the way in which the husband and wife divided or shared the household tasks. We called a task autonomous when it was performed chiefly or entirely by either the husband or wife, and shared when it was performed

by both together most of the time or regarded it as a common responsibility. This gave us three categories: husband's share, wife's
share, and common share. Since ordinarily fathers do not, and are
not expected to, participate much in household tasks, rather modest increments in the proportion of tasks performed by the father
affected the classification far more than did such variations in the
mothers' patterns.

We were able to identify four typical ways in which the
families divided household tasks between husband and wife:

The balanced family was one in which the husband took
responsibility for at least 18 per cent of the tasks and shared at least
another 15 per cent with his wife. Ordinarily, this family approxi-
mated in its division of labor a 20–20–60 balance, with the husband taking responsibility for 20 per cent and sharing another 20
per cent of the tasks. The distinctive characteristic of this type of
family was its balance between role articulation, in which the husband and wife are distinguished by distinct tasks and task areas,
and sharing, in which the husband and wife work together and
took common responsibility. The father in the typical balanced
family took full responsibility for all traditionally male tasks. In
addition, he assumed responsibility for a few other household tasks
such as carrying out the garbage, and, for at least one child, performed a care task. Fathers in this group shared with their wives a
large number of child care tasks, and some took full responsibility
for 30 per cent of them.

The sharing family was one in which the father's participation was almost entirely on a sharing level. A family was placed in
this category if the father took responsibility for less than 18 per
cent of the tasks and shared more than 15 per cent of them. Usually, these fathers took responsibility for about 12 per cent and
shared over 33 per cent of the tasks. The distinctive mark of this
type of family was lack of role differentiation, or role confusion.
Even when these fathers did take responsibility for tasks, they did
not do so in a particular area, and the wives shared in roughly half
of the traditional male tasks. Frequently, the husbands and wives
in these families shared more tasks than they performed separately;

in a few cases the proportion shared was as high as 90 per cent, with the husband sharing responsibility for all the traditional wife's tasks, such as making beds and cooking meals.

The traditional family was one in which the father participated in almost no household tasks. He took responsibility for less than 18 per cent and shared less than 15 per cent of the tasks. Ordinarily, he took responsibility for about 16 per cent and shared another 10 per cent of the tasks. The distinctive mark of these families was the very small amount of sharing and therefore the high degree of role segregation. In this type of family the male and female roles were clearly distinct, but there was little linkage between them. In some of these families the men did no household tasks at all, and in others they took a fair amount of responsibility, but in no case did they share many tasks.

The unconventional family was one in which the father did as much as the mother, or more. It was marked by very little participation by the mothers, some of whom did less than 20 per cent of the household tasks. When the father does more housework than the mother, it is clear that they have reversed the traditional roles and that their family organization contradicts cultural expectations.

Table 17 presents the numbers and percentages of each type of family and the average percentage of household tasks performed and shared by husband and wife.

Table 17

FAMILIES' DIVISION OF LABOR

Type	N	Percentage	Percentage of tasks performed by:		
			Husband	Both	Wife
Balanced	32	41.6	20	20	60
Sharing	28	36.4	12	34	54
Traditional	12	15.5	16	10	74
Unconventional	5	6.5	41	24	35
Total	77	100.00			

We were interested in finding out what relationships, if any, existed between the division of labor and other characteristics of the family, particularly the relationships and emotional health of the members.

We were able to use only two measures of the degree of love and affection between the husband and wife: our own subjective assessments of their relationship and the data they contributed on their sexual life. In both cases we were limited to the twenty-eight families that had been most intensively studied—that is, the eight families in the pilot study plus the families of the ten most healthy and ten most disturbed subjects in the larger study. The data on the frequency of sexual intercourse and on the couple's increasing or decreasing enjoyment in the sexual relation during the course of their marriage are probably the most reliable since they are independent of the observers' judgments.

When we examine the relationship between the division of labor in the family and the reported frequency of sexual intercourse between husband and wife, we find that ten of the thirteen balanced couples, two of the eight sharing couples, and none of the six traditional couples reported that they had intercourse frequently. Similarly, increasing satisfaction with sex relations was reported by seven out of eight balanced couples, three out of four sharing, and one out of five traditional couples. The sole family from this group with an unconventional division of labor reported that their sex relations were infrequent, but that they experienced increasing satisfaction.

Though it would be folly to suggest that a satisfactory sexual relationship is essential to a happy marriage, it is undoubtedly true that this is ordinarily the case, and that the sexual relationship of the couple probably reflects their affection and respect for each other. We found that the balanced family has the most frequent and satisfying sexual relationship, and the traditional family the least frequent and satisfying. We interpret this to mean that the distinct responsibilities and tasks in the balanced family provide a differentiation of sexual identity, a way of contributing to the family, and a means of care, and the shared tasks provide the couple with regular structured interactions and a set of common experiences.

We also evaluated the success of the marriage in terms of the extent to which the relationship between the husband and wife was one of affection and respect, without any significant amount of destructive interaction. If we felt that the partners were enthusiastic about their marriage and their mates, we rated the marriage as good. If they were satisfied, but either lacked enthusiasm or indicated that there were some serious disappointments in the mate, we rated the marriage as fair. If the marriage was without affection or the partners had no respect for each other, or interacted in a destructive manner, we rated the marriage as bad. As in the case of sexual frequency and satisfaction, our data were such that we could make these evaluations only for the twenty-eight families that we had studied most intensively. Table 18 presents the relationship between the success of the marriage and the division of labor.

Table 18

DIVISION OF LABOR AND SUCCESS OF MARRIAGE

| | Success of marriage | | |
Type	Good	Fair	Bad
Balanced	7	5	1
Sharing	2	5	1
Traditional	0	3	3
Unconventional	1	0	0

No causal relationship should be imputed, for it may well be that the couple who are compatible seek out the balanced pattern, whereas the couple who have become estranged reflect this fact in their household life, the husband refusing to do anything at all. This may be the case. However, we are inclined to see this relationship between compatibility and division of labor as reciprocal. There are clearly forces outside the personalities of the husband and wife, such as the patterns they knew as children, the degree to which the family is integrated into the community (Bott, 1957) and their economic position, that shape the pattern of their division of labor. But once formed, this pattern can help or aggravate the couple's relationship, and this, we believe, is its basic significance.

PARENTS' EMOTIONAL HEALTH

It has become increasingly apparent that the matrix of interpersonal relationships, particularly in primary groups like the family, is of utmost significance to the personality. In fact it has been suggested that the personality as a system may actually mesh with the intimate small social systems of which it is a part. This approach views emotional health as a combination of personality and small social system. Our research supports this view.

We examined the relationship between the emotional health of the parents and the division of labor that they had set up in their families. It can be seen that none of the healthiest husbands or wives are found among the traditional or unconventional families. These patterns are clearly not compatible with emotional health. On the other hand, it seems that the balanced pattern is most compatible with emotional health in husbands and wives, though many healthy women also chose the sharing pattern.

Our data indicated that among the sixteen emotionally healthy men, 69 per cent chose the balanced, 31 per cent the sharing, and none the traditional or unconventional divisions of labor. Among the nineteen emotionally healthy women, 54 per cent chose the balanced, 46 per cent the sharing, and none the traditional or unconventional. The emotionally disturbed husbands and wives chose the balanced, sharing, and traditional patterns in almost equal proportions.

What is the explanation of these results? We assume that health is not compatible with the traditional or unconventional patterns because they are most in conflict with the norms of society. In the accepted social pattern the mother does most of the housework, but the father helps. In the traditional family the husband and wife share almost nothing. They must be alienated from each other. In the unconventional family the husband does so much housework that the community deems him effeminate. The balanced pattern is compatible with health in the husband since with this pattern he can maintain a distinctive status in the home and also share certain experiences with his wife. The sharing pattern, however, gives him no unique role in the family. This pattern is more successful for the wife, because it permits her to have a combination of individual and shared tasks. Nevertheless, the dominant pattern for both healthy men and women is the balanced one.

In interpreting the significance of these results one should note that the judgments of emotional health and the specifications of the division of labor were entirely independent. The family's division of labor was objectively scored by a team of sociologists. The judgments of health and illness were made entirely independently by the psychiatrist and psychologist, so there was no contamination.

CHILDREN'S EMOTIONAL HEALTH

While the relationship of the division of labor to the emotional health of the parents is probably reciprocal, presumably its relationship to the emotional health of the children is one of cause and effect. In the first place, the example of appropriate sex roles helps children to accept their own sexuality, to be secure in their sexual identity, and to identify with their own bodies. This learning is certainly facilitated by parents who play distinct and culturally appropriate sex roles. It is furthered, too, by the parent who leads the child of the opposite sex to a comprehension of heterosexuality, within safe limits. Second, the pilot study demonstrated that if the husband and wife have a good relationship they meet each other's needs in such a way that their own psychopathologies are not passed on to the children. Finally, the family as an organization benefits from an efficient division of labor—one in which there is sufficient differentiation in responsibilities to assure that the work gets done and at the same time sufficient sharing to provide a basis of common experience. Table 19 shows the relationship between the division of labor in the family and the emotional health of the children.

The difference between the proportion of emotionally healthy children in the balanced family and that in all the other types is striking. Clearly, this type of family is advantageous for the development of emotional health in children. It produces approximately twice as many healthy and half as many disturbed children as do

Table 19

DIVISION OF LABOR AND EMOTIONAL HEALTH OF CHILDREN

	Emotional health			
Type	Percentage healthy	Percentage intermediate	Percentage disturbed	N
Balanced	49	22	29	(68)
Sharing	20	25	55	(64)
Traditional	9	27	64	(22)
Unconventional	0	0	100	(5)

the other two major types. It is possible, of course, that this relationship is really a product of the greater concentration of emotionally healthy parents in this type of family. To test this, we held the emotional health of the parents constant by dividing our families into those with emotionally disturbed parents and those with emotionally healthy parents and then recomputing the proportions of healthy and sick children in each type of family. We did this for the father and mother separately. It can be seen that though the emotional health of the parents does influence the emotional health of the children, the relationship between the type of family and the emotional health of the children persists independently. (See Table 20.) Thus while the disturbance of parents tends to increase the proportion of disturbed and decrease the proportion of healthy children, the balanced family continues to produce the highest proportion of healthy and the lowest proportion of disturbed children.

Since we had given each of the original subjects the MMPI masculinity-femininity scale (on which a high score indicates sexual problems), we were able to compare the scores of children from sharing families with those of children from all the others. The girls showed no difference in their scores, but the boys from sharing families scored definitely higher on this scale than the boys from other types of families.

The average scores for boys from different types of families: Balanced (fifteen boys)—23.5; Sharing (fourteen boys)—28; and Traditional (six boys)—24. Nine of the fifteen boys from balanced

Table 20

Emotional Health of Children and Parents

Type	All families	Percentage of healthy children with:			
		Disturbed father	Healthy father	Disturbed mother	Healthy mother
Balanced	49	40	66	30	68
Sharing	20	24.5	40	18	25
Traditional	9	10	—	9	—
Unconventional	0	0	—	0	—

Type	All families	Percentage of disturbed children with:			
		Disturbed father	Healthy father	Disturbed mother	Healthy mother
Balanced	29	40	15	48	11
Sharing	55	60	30	56	50
Traditional	64	62	—	60	—
Unconventional	100	100	0	100	—

families and only two of the fourteen boys from sharing families scored 23 or lower. Nine of the boys from sharing families and only two of the boys from balanced families scored 26 or higher. The contrast between the scores of the boys from these two kinds of families is quite sharp. We can presume, then, that boys from sharing families were more threatened by confused sexual identity than boys from the other types of families.

RELATIONSHIPS WITHIN FAMILY

Other data from the interviewers' reports about the families in each group that were studied intensively, either because they were part of the pilot study or because they were part of the two extreme groups, revealed striking differences between the internal relationships in the different types of families.

The interaction between husband and wife in the traditional families was minimal, and usually destructive. These husbands and wives lived remote from each other, with no love or respect for each other. We found despair, barely constrained hostility, and a sense of emptiness in their family lives. Parents and children neither respected nor enjoyed being with each other.

Among the sharing families we immediately noticed a definite but sometimes aberrant relationship between the husband and wife. Where the relationship seemed warm and close, it showed clear signs of psychopathology. In general, the family had little family life; the parents and children were not close, and the family seldom functioned as a group, and when it did, not happily. In only one family did the parents and children seem to enjoy being together. Often one of the children was remote from the rest of the family or one of the parents, and seen as a problem. The closeness in sharing families was usually only between the parents.

The dominant mark of the balanced families was the strong and warm bond between all the members of the family. Parents and children respected and enjoyed being with each other. While this was not true of all of the balanced families, it was true of ten of the fourteen we knew well, and it was true of none of the sharing or the traditional families.

Since personality must in some measure represent the internalization of emotional relationships in the family, it is to be expected that the division and sharing of housework—the most apparent and routinized of emotional relationships in the family—will profoundly affect the personalities of the children. Our findings support this hypothesis.

Traditional families are often empty and frightening, and so, inevitably, are personalities of the children who internalize their characteristic relationships as models for dealing with themselves and their worlds. These children carry a heavy burden. For them most problems, particularly personal problems, are insoluble, sex is frightening, the sex role is threatening and confusing, and trust is unknown.

In contrast, our model balanced family is a warm and pleasant environment nurturing lives secure and full of positive experiences. Children in these families see parents who are obviously fond of each other, who enjoy spending time together, and who have something to exchange and something to share in the framework of household tasks. The children feel themselves part of this warm and positive relationship. While many of these families face problems, they show no doubt about their ability to solve them. Such children can and do face life with the expectation of rich rewards to be found in intimate social relationships, with an almost unshakable trust in people and in the blessings of marriage, and with confidence in themselves as people and in their attractiveness as men or women.

Between the emptiness and hostility of the traditional family and the warmth and integration of the balanced family, one finds the sharing family. Here, though there is a positive relationship between the parents, it is not the same warm, close, and loving relationship found in the balanced family. The children in these families hardly seem a part of them, and one gets no sense of enjoyment of the family as a whole or of rich emotional bonds. Finally, they face problems in self-esteem and sexual identity because they live in a family world in which they lack a place and which offers no clear definition of sex roles or acceptance of sexuality.

We interpret these findings as indicating that the use and distribution of family work structures and facilitates the communication of emotions. We see work as the instrument of care, and care the reality of love. Couples who work for each other and their children are demonstrating their love and respect. Distinctive tasks and responsibilities provide both the means for demonstrating love and the basis for individuality and esteem. Yet at the same time some kind of sharing is also necessary to maintain interaction and provide a sense of common life.

When both autonomy and sharing are present, the need for care and the need for interaction are met. The families who follow this pattern seem to be closest and happiest, to have the most successful marriages, the most satisfactory sex lives, and the largest proportion of emotionally healthy parents and children. We call this the balanced family. Fortunately, it seems to be the most prevalent type in our sample.

When there is a deficiency in either autonomy or sharing, a corresponding deficiency appears in the life of the family. A deficiency in sharing, which is manifested in the traditional family, means that there is very little interaction between the husband and wife, that they have little in common, that they have a poor sex life, and that their children tend to be emotionally disturbed. Finally, when there is no autonomy, as in the sharing family, the husband and wife lack the means for demonstrating love and respect for each other; they seem more like siblings than husband and wife, and hence, as one might expect, have little or no sexual relationship. Their children tend to be emotionally disturbed.

Work, then, is not something separate from emotional life, but an integral part of it and, through it, of the personalities and emotional health of the family members.

CHAPTER **8**

Family Roles

Most social organizations can be described in terms of established roles, which are ordinarily functionally related to the ends of the group or the needs of the members. In this chapter we describe the family as a system of social roles, restricting our attention to the three main roles played by the parents: the work role, involving duties like earning a living or doing the housework; the parental role, involving the care and discipline of the children; and the spouse role, involving the parents' relationship with each other, including their sexual relationship. We focused our attention on the parents' acceptance of their various family roles, rather than on the content of the roles themselves, because we suspected that the success of the family's functioning is related to the extent to which the parents accept and successfully perform their three family roles.

To test this belief we developed a crude scale of role ac-

ceptance and performance with which we first graded each parent.
It was then possible, by using the emotional health of the children
as the criterion variable, to determine whether the degree of role
acceptance had any effect on the successful functioning of the
family. Role acceptance was scored by the sociologist and emotional health by the psychologist and psychiatrist. The judgments
were all made independently of each other.

ROLE ACCEPTANCE

Our fundamental question was: Does this man or woman
accept and enjoy his or her family roles? For example, does the
man feel satisfied with his job or does he feel that it is a frustrating
or boring necessity? If the latter is the case, there is a good chance
that he may blame his family, feeling that if he did not have these
obligations, he could easily change to something else. Whether or
not this is in fact the case makes little difference, for if the man be-
lieves it to be real, it is, to paraphrase Thomas (1924), real in its
consequence upon his family. Similarly, it seems that many modern
housewives are deeply dissatisfied with their role, finding it boring
and to some extent degrading. Again it seems highly likely that if
this is the case, there are unpleasant consequences for the family.
A person who finds his work role unsatisfactory is diminished in
his life, perhaps to a considerable extent, for work consumes a large
and important part of his time.

Work is the only one of the parental role areas in our
study that appears to be unrelated to the emotional health of the
children. While it is true that fathers who are completely satisfied
with their work do seem to have a greater tendency to have emotionally healthy children than fathers who are dissatisfied, both the
differences and the sample size are too small to rule out the operations of chance. Beyond this we found no real difference in the
number of emotionally healthy or disturbed children in families
in which the parents were satisfied and those in which they were
not satisfied with their work.

In general, as might be expected, the men who were happy
and satisfied with their work were those who were successful, and
vice versa. The fathers in our sample were managers, lawyers, sales-

men, skilled workers, dentists, artists, accountants, doctors, and
service officers. The satisfied ones said things like:

> I am very happy in my work. I believe that I made my
> job into what I wanted it to be, and I am really enjoying it
> now. My work is tremendously important to me.
> I am on my way to achieving my goals. I have achieved
> recognition and honors in my profession. . . . It involves inter-
> esting problems which require ingenuity to work out.
> I like my work. . . . I have always been a salesman and
> liked it. . . . I find my greatest satisfaction when I am selling.
> I don't run away from other things [parts of his job] but I
> don't enjoy them nearly as much.

The dissatisfied made statements like:

> Well, sometimes there is not much satisfaction, but I
> think it is the contact with the men I work with. You are
> achieving something as in most jobs, I guess, and then you have
> to earn a living.
> I feel that I was foolish not to have moved five years
> ago, but maybe it's just bad luck, if you want to put it that
> way. I don't think anyone is ever satisfied, not completely.
> I'm quite frankly going on the shelf. The organization
> is changing. . . . I'm one of the old timers . . . but it's one of
> those things. What can I do about it? I've got to accept it.

All the men who made statements like this were, in fact,
failures. Actually, these two groups of statements do not represent
the extremes; more than 50 per cent of the men were satisfied with
their work, about 20 per cent were clearly dissatisfied, and the remainder either noncommittal or ambivalent. Our data indicated
that there are almost no differences in the proportions of emotionally healthy and emotionally disturbed children in the families of
fathers who had high, intermediate, and low acceptance of their
work roles.

The same pattern held for the mother's work, though the
findings were less conclusive since a large number of the mothers
seemed to have ambivalent feelings about housework. Most of

them neither complained nor showed enthusiasm; they appeared
to feel that some parts of the work were interesting, but that it all
had to be done and that it was not too onerous. Those in the extremes were a distinct minority. The satisfied made statements like:

> I am fastidious about my house and keeping things clean.
> I like what I am doing—keeping house, getting meals, and so
> forth.
> I really enjoy it. I make pickles and things that I don't
> have to. I knit.
> Yes, I do like it. Of course, I am a very methodical per-
> son. I really enjoy getting at the cupboards and putting them
> in apple-pie order. I do this to a fault.

The dissatisfied tended to be laconic and to show their dissatisfaction by using their time for other things and by leaving the
house pretty much to the rest of the family. Those who did express
themselves made statements like:

> What pleased me most was to find that I could get into
> business. I don't like housework and never did.
> I definitely don't believe that just because you are a
> woman you should be the only one who does the work, just be-
> cause you are a housewife.

A comparison of the proportions of emotionally healthy and
disturbed children in the families of mothers who had high, intermediate, or low acceptance of their work roles reveals no difference.

Again, there appears to be little relationship between the
parent's attitude toward work role and the emotional health of the
children. Why did we not find the association that we expected?
It may be that our questions did not probe deeply enough into
attitudes. However, we hypothesize that though actual malfunc-
tioning in the work area does have serious emotional consequences
for the family, as demonstrated in Chapter Five, the attitudes of
the parents toward their work are only significant when they affect
their relationship with each other or the children, or when they

affect their performance of their work. Though there is some association between attitudes and successful performance of work roles, particularly among men, the relationship is not perfect.

When we speak of parents' accepting their parental role, we mean that they really enjoy the children, both being with them and looking after them. Dissatisfaction with the role is expressed in an effort to avoid the children, or to spend a minimum amount of time with them.

Mothers who had most fully accepted their role described in detail and with interest and enthusiasm their relationships with their various children. Ordinarily, they spent considerable time with their children, sometimes even putting aside certain parts of the day for listening to and talking with their older children. They seemed to have a sensitive appreciation of their children and were able to express this concern and understanding to the interviewers. It should be noted, however, that a mother's relationship was not the same with all of her children; some mothers gave very different responses to questions about different children. One mother said of a son, "Oh, he is a joy. He has a lovely disposition. He is very affectionate. He is very open with me. He is one of those satisfactory children." Of another son she said, "He is a good boy, believe me. I can trust him; he never holds anything back from me——Poor——He was kind of an experiment." This mother had quite different attitudes toward these two sons, and for the first we scored her high in the mother role, for she enjoyed the boy and liked to spend time with him, but for the second we scored her low, for she felt guilty about him, was harsh with him, and generally did not enjoy her relationship to him. Her total score was thus a compromise.

In some cases the mothers did feel differently toward different children but seemed to be able to maintain a positive attitude toward them all. Here is how one such mother reacted to her son and daughter: "I may sound like a proud parent, but I think —— has something. I hope he will make a contribution to the world. I feel that he has something to give—nothing big, but something." Then speaking of her daughter: "I don't mean that she does not have anything to give, but I feel her destiny and happiness lie in being a wife and mother." This mother got a very high score for her son and a medium score for her daughter.

Generally, it was easy to differentiate those mothers who scored high in role acceptance from those who scored low, for, surprisingly, the latter expressed quite clearly their feelings of avoidance and the ways in which they rejected the children they did not like. For example, one mother spoke of her son in this way: "He has always been kind of the negative one in the family. From the time he was fifteen months he was negative. He has no assurance. Yet he is quite stubborn within the family as to what he thinks. He is quite lazy——I can't discuss anything with him that pertains to what he wants to do or what he likes to do. He is quite selfish and tries to be independent."

We gave great emphasis to the time the mothers actually spent with their children as evidence of their acceptance of their parental roles. Our data show conclusively that the mother's acceptance of her parental role has considerable impact on the emotional health of her children. Almost all of the children of mothers who had thoroughly accepted their parental role were healthy, whereas almost all of the children of mothers who had not were disturbed.

We used the same criteria to judge how well the father accepted his role as parent. As might be expected, many fathers invested much of their emotional lives in their work, so that there were many more fathers than mothers whom we rated low. Nevertheless, our data again show that the relationship between acceptance of parental role and emotional health of the children is close, but not quite as close for the father as for the mother. Again, the father's acceptance is also important: almost all of the children of accepting fathers were healthy, whereas many of the children of the others were not.

It seems possible that these scores reflect how close a social and emotional relationship the parent is actually maintaining with his child, as well as how much he accepts and likes him. What happens when both parents accept or reject their parental roles can be seen in Table 21, where we have combined the parents' acceptance ratings. For the purpose of convenience we have used the actual scores, which run from 5, or complete acceptance, to 1, or complete rejection. In the table 5 means 4 and 5, and 1 means 1 and 2.

Table 21
BOTH PARENTS' ACCEPTANCE OF PARENTAL ROLES AND
EMOTIONAL HEALTH OF CHILDREN

Emotional health	Acceptance of parental roles					
	5&5	5&3	5&1	3&3	3&1	1&1
Healthy	6	7	4	2	0	1
Intermediate	1	2	0	0	2	1
Disturbed	0	5	2	3	4	5

The presence of two accepting parents seems an assurance of health, for none of the children from such families were disturbed. But the presence of even one accepting parent is important: Of the twenty healthy children in this sample, seventeen had at least one fully accepting parent. If the children have one accepting parent, then even if the other is fully rejecting, most children seem to remain healthy. But in the families in which one parent completely rejected the children and the other did not strongly accept them, nine of the thirteen children were disturbed and only one was healthy. In such families the child is psychologically trapped: He is forced into a self-concept of worthlessness at the same time that he is deprived of the interaction with his parents that makes growth and everyday life rewarding. His problems mount and are seemingly without solution. No wonder the result is emotional illness.

Though we believe these findings are accurate and discerning, they are judgments. Therefore we supplemented them with a more quantitative and less subjective estimation of the relationship between the degree to which the mother and father participated in the care of the children and the children's emotional health. We asked if the father or mother did each of certain tasks often, sometimes, or never. For one the parent did often he received a score of 3, for one he did sometimes, a score of 1. The tasks were as follows:

Infant care:
Cares for sick child
Bathes child
Puts child to bed
Feeds child
Gets up if child cries at night

Child care:
Teaches table manners
Reads or tells stories
Gets child up in the morning
Helps with homework
Participates in hobbies
Participates in sports

We then ran product-moment correlations on the relationship between the total scores of each of the parents and the emotional health of children, the emotional health of boys, the emotional health of girls and, finally, the scores of boys and girls on thirty-eight psychological scales. Only the father's participation in the care of infants and the mother's participation in the care of the children showed any relationship to the psychological states of the children.

The father's participation in care of infants was correlated: * plus .494 (n-24) significant at .02 level with emotional health of girls; plus .571 (n-22) significant at .02 level with sociability in girls (CPI-Sy); plus .505 (n-22) significant at .02 level with ego strength in girls (MMPI-Es); plus 4.33 (n-22) significant at .05 level with dominance-confidence in girls (Vassar-Dc); plus .428 (n-22) significant at .05 level with dominance in girls (CPI-D). His participation showed no correlation with either the emotional health (plus .052) or the psychological test scores of boys.

Since these correlations were limited to the subjects in the major study and did not include the subjects in the pilot study or the siblings in either study, we also ran cross-tabulations including these other children. (See Table 22.)

A direct relationship between the emotional health of girls and their father's participation in the care of infants is clear. Of the daughters of fathers who scored high on participation 52 per

* The use of correlation coefficient and tests of significance is limited to those cases where standardized psychological scales were used. Only in those cases did we feel that such tests were appropriate to the kind of data we had.

Table 22

PARTICIPATION OF FATHER IN INFANT CARE AND EMOTIONAL HEALTH OF BOYS AND GIRLS

Boys						
Emotional	High		Medium		Low	
Health	N	%	N	%	N	%
Healthy	(7)	32	(8)	25	(7)	24
Intermed.	(4)	18	(11)	34	(6)	21
Disturbed	(11)	50	(13)	41	(16)	55
Total	(22)	100	(32)	100	(29)	100

Girls						
Emotional	High		Medium		Low	
health	N	%	N	%	N	%
Healthy	(12)	52	(6)	26	(10)	30
Intermed.	(5)	22	(6)	26	(6)	18
Disturbed	(6)	26	(11)	48	(17)	52
Total	(23)	100	(23)	100	(33)	100

cent were healthy, whereas 52 per cent of the daughters of fathers who scored low were disturbed. Conversely, there still appears to be no relationship between the father's participation in infant care and the emotional health of boys.

Similarly, the mother's participation in child care was correlated: plus .404 (n-45) significant at .01 level with emotional health of boys; .403 (n-39) significant at .01 level with ascendance in boys (G-Z-A); .386 (n-35) significant at .05 level with hypomania (MMPI-Ma); .346 (n-35) significant at .05 level with sociability (CPI-Sy); .340 (n-35) significant at .05 level with self-acceptance (CPI-Sa); minus .351 (n-35) significant at .05 level with introversion (MMPI-Si).

Cross-tabulations including the siblings of our subjects and the children from the pilot study produced the results in Table 23. Since the number of cases in categories of low participation is very small, these results should be taken with reservations.

Table 23

PARTICIPATION OF MOTHER IN CHILD CARE AND
EMOTIONAL HEALTH OF BOYS AND GIRLS

Emotional Health	Boys					
	High		Medium		Low	
	N	%	N	%	N	%
Healthy	(5)	45	(12)	20	(0)	0
Intermed.	(2)	19	(17)	31	(0)	0
Disturbed	(4)	36	(26)	49	(8)	100
Total	(11)	100	(55)	100	(8)	100

Emotional health	Girls					
	High		Medium		Low	
	N	%	N	%	N	%
Healthy	(6)	60	(11)	24	(2)	33
Intermed.	(2)	20	(9)	19	(1)	19
Disturbed	(2)	20	(26)	57	(3)	48
Total	(10)	100	(46)	100	(6)	100

It is probably true that the correlations, which test for differences within the central group, are a more accurate reflection of the relationship. Nevertheless, the findings that all of the sons of mothers scoring low on participation were disturbed and that most of the sons and daughters of mothers scoring high were healthy, are of considerable interest. These differences in the extremes are not, of course, apparent in the correlations.

The participation of the parent of the opposite sex in the care and rearing of the child seems to be critical to the emotional health of the child. Thus we find that the participation of the father in the care of his infant children is closely related to the emotional health of his daughters but not his sons. The more he takes part in infant care, the more likely are his daughters to be outgoing, enterprising, ingenious (CPI-Sy), aggressive, confident, persistent, and planful (CPI-Do and Vassar-D, C)', and to have

stronger egos (MMPI-Es). If the father plays no part in the care
of his daughters, they are likely to have the opposite characteristics.
But none of this applies to sons.

The boys are more likely to be affected by their mother's
participation. We found that the more the mother participated in
the care of older children (there was little or no difference in the
degree to which mothers participated in the care of younger children) the more likely their sons were to be healthy, outgoing, enterprising, and ingenious (CPI-Sy and MMPI-Si), to dominate
others (G-Z-1A), to demonstrate marked productivity in thought
and action, and to be self-confident and enjoy a sense of personal
worth (CPI-Sa). Curiously, neither the emotional health ratings
nor any of the personality scales of girls were correlated at a significant level of probability with the degree of the mother's participation. However, the cross-tabulations using the larger group of
girls do show a mild relationship between their emotional health
and their mothers' participation. We are inclined, however, to accept the fact that the participation of mothers and fathers in child-
rearing is particularly important to the children of the opposite sex.
But why?

PSYCHODYNAMICS OF HETEROSEXUALITY

Let us first consider the case of the father. Our findings are
that his sharing in the care of the children at all ages is closely related to the emotional health of girls but not boys. This is particularly true during infancy, though we should point out that fathers
who give a hand with infants usually continue later on. This is important; indeed, we think that it is the care during this later period
that permits the father and daughter to work out, within an already formed relationship, the psychodynamics of heterosexuality.

In the growth of the child the development of a sound sexual identity involves two major, closely interrelated axes: that of
identifying with an adult of the same sex, and that of learning to
relate to and be accepted by the opposite sex. For the girl, the
mother fulfills the first need. The child identifies with her because
of her power and similarity, and because of pressures brought to
bear by the family. However, her ability to do so depends on her

relationship to her mother, the distinctiveness of the role played by the mother in the family, and the father's acceptance of her and her mother as attractive females.

The second need, that of learning to relate to and be accepted by the opposite sex, is one that, for the girl, is met primarily by the father. But incest taboos make it a delicate and sensitive matter. Essentially, the little girl has to find some way of presenting herself sexually to the father without offending against the taboos. If the family is sufficiently puritanical or fearful of sex for any reason, it immediately represses, and thus causes her to suppress the very earliest signs of it, and the suppression will persist and cause problems in adult life. However, even if the family is—as most modern families seem to be—relatively tolerant and understanding about sexuality, the little girl's relationship to her father will still be difficult. She may make relatively overt, though not necessarily conscious, sexual advances to her father—by snuggling, kissing, hugging, or lying beside or on top of him; in other words, using her limited and as yet native vocabulary of gestures she will present herself sexually. When this happens—and of course it happens in hundreds of little ways in the daily life of a family—it creates a critical situation for the father. He must somehow reassure his little girl that she is an acceptable person and an attractive female, without returning the sexuality of her advances. If he is frightened by her advances and rejects her, she has had a lesson in the evils of femininity and her own unattractiveness. If he accepts and returns her advances in a kind of playful amorousness, she can become frightened, for this may be more than she wanted, and she is well aware that her father belongs to her mother. However, if the father has already established a firm relationship of play and care, he can and will turn these advances into established and safe channels of play and she will not find herself rejected. In other words, fathers who have taken a share in the care of their daughters since infancy are best able to accept them as females, and these daughters have an assurance of their own worth in the eyes of the important male in their world.

In addition, it should be noted that there is bound to be a certain amount of eroticism, using this term in its most generalized sense, in the handling of infants. We can assume it is bound to enter into the body contact in bathing, carrying, and playing with the baby, and that the reciprocal delight of parent and baby in these contacts has something of this character. It is possible, therefore, that the father who cares for his infant daughter has already communicated his acceptance of her as a physical being, expressing it in his delight in her soft and cuddly qualities. It must be that this delight in the daughter is communicated to her, so that she gains an assurance that males like and accept her, if not as a female, at least as a physical being. As the daughter grows older and makes more overt advances to her father, she can handle these within the framework of the existing relationship, for, since she already has the sense of her own acceptability to males, his failure to accept or return her advances will not be interpreted by her as a rejection of herself as a female.

The contrast with the father who has not taken a hand in the care of his daughter as an infant or as a child is striking. In this case, if the small girl's advances are rejected, the rejection may be very destructive of her sense of her own acceptability and identity. If her advances are accepted, there may develop too close and eroticized (though we assume nongenital) a relationship, which is bound to frighten her or to make it difficult for her to achieve independence.

In these circumstances it is not surprising that the father who shares in the care of his daughter as an infant tends to have an emotionally healthy daughter, whereas the father who does not care for his daughter (and we mean the term in its double sense) tends to have an emotionally disturbed one.

There is, of course, a parallel in the mother's relationship to her sons. Normally, she is closely involved in the care of all her children as infants (as were all the mothers in our sample). Thus she is likely to have established early the close emotional relationship with her son that gives to him a sense of his worth and his physical acceptability by the most important member of the opposite sex. However, there is incongruity between the mother's treatment of her son as a child and as a man. Her problem is to change the relationship to one of respect and care as he grows from infant to child. She may find it difficult not to over-respond to his more overt sexual advances in childhood, though she may be so frightened of sexuality that her rejection of them is severe and alarming. Her transfer of care to the more grown-up aspects of the relationship—teaching table manners, helping with homework, being a spectator or partner in his sports—offers a way of continuing the relationship without overeroticization or rejection. We maintain that this is the only successful way for the mother to handle the heterosexual aspects of the relationship with her son.

We see the role of spouse as having many facets, among them companion, sex partner, and need-satisfier. Here, however, we treat this role in terms of companionship and sexuality. In general, we have noticed that where the partners have a good sexual relationship they are also good companions; but it is also possible for them to be good companions and have a very poor sexual relationship.

We asked for information about the sex lives of husband and wife from only twenty-eight families (nine in the pilot study and nineteen in the major study). Husband and wife were each asked about frequency of intercourse and their satisfaction with their sexual relationships over the period of the marriage. The couples varied considerably. (See Table 24.) A few remained very active, having intercourse from ten to—in one case—over twenty times a month.

Table 24

MONTHLY FREQUENCY OF INTERCOURSE

Frequency	Number of couples
20 plus	1
15–19	0
10–14	4
7–9	2
4–6	4
1–3	16
0	1

In many of the couples, all in their fifties, there was very little sexual activity. Fifteen of them in the 1–3 category had intercourse twice a month or less, and where couples reported such a low frequency we felt that they were probably overestimating. Thus over half of the couples in this sample had abandoned intercourse as a major source of gratification. This probably reflects the widespread inhibitions and emotional problems of middle-class Protestant couples, at least in our society, with sexuality.

Yet the matter remains of considerable importance, as the following tables relating sexuality to emotional health show. For the purpose of these cross-tabulations we call frequencies of four or more times a month frequent and the rest infrequent. The scores in Table 25 represent the most conservative of the frequencies claimed by the husband or the wife.

Table 25

FREQUENCY OF INTERCOURSE AND EMOTIONAL
HEALTH IN FAMILY

Frequency reported by couple	Emotional health[a]								
	Husband			Wife			Children		
	H	I	D	H	I	D	H	I	D
Frequent	4	3	4	7	2	2	17	2	4
Infrequent	5	1	11	3	4	10	14	9	17

[a] H = Healthy; I = Intermediate; D = Disturbed.

Two observations can be made from these cross-tabulations. First, we can assume that the sexual activity of the couple is in some measure a consequence of their emotional health, for only four out of fifteen disturbed husbands and two out of twelve disturbed wives had intercourse four or more times a month. However, it can also be seen that emotional health is no guarantee of an ample sex life. The cross-tabulations suggest that though frequent intercourse tends to indicate emotional health, infrequent intercourse does not necessarily indicate emotional illness. This is corroborated by our own case material, for we found families in which the husband and wife had a very poor sexual relationship, but were otherwise happy and contented with each other and had emotionally healthy children. However, where they did have a good sexual relationship this usually, but not always, meant a good relationship on other levels and emotionally healthy children.

Table 26

SEXUAL SATISFACTION AND EMOTIONAL HEALTH
IN FAMILY

Reported sexual satisfaction	Emotional health[a]								
	Father			Mother			Child		
	H	I	D	H	I	D	H	I	D
Increasing	5	1	5	7	2	2	16	5	5
Stable	2	1	5	1	1	6	9	2	9
Decreasing	0	1	6	1	2	4	2	2	8

[a] H = Healthy; I = Intermediate; D = Disturbed.

It can be seen that healthy fathers and mothers reported increasing satisfaction in intercourse over the period of their marriage, whereas disturbed fathers and mothers reported their satisfaction to be either stable or decreasing. Congruent with our findings about the relationship between the parents' frequency of intercourse and the emotional health of the children is the finding that parents who experienced increasing satisfaction tended to have healthy children and those who felt decreasing satisfaction tended to have disturbed children. It is, of course, highly probable that those who experienced increasing satisfaction from sexual intercourse sought it more frequently than those who did not, so that the congruency of these two sets of findings is to be expected. In view of the infrequency of intercourse reported by most of the couples we must conclude that the report of stable satisfaction must in many instances be a report of little or none. From our knowledge of these families we would conclude that only those reporting increasing satisfaction were, in fact, really enjoying intercourse—that is, of twenty-eight couples reporting, only eleven, or approximately 40 per cent.

In interpreting these findings one important fact should be kept in mind: The twenty-eight families included the families of the ten most disturbed of the seventy-nine subjects in the major study and eighteen families drawn from the very healthiest group. It is thus difficult to estimate how far these findings should be generalized.

The picture emerges of a group of families in which many of the husbands and wives were more often than not uneasy in their sexual identity, experiencing difficulties in finding sexual satisfaction, and generally beginning to avoid intercourse. While a sizable proportion enjoyed an active and satisfactory sex life, the large number of those who did not indicates the prevalence of sexual conflict in our society.

We judged spouses' companionship by the extent to which they looked forward to each other's company and enjoyed talking and being together. This was not necessarily the same thing as actually doing things together, a matter that depended somewhat on the occupation of the father; some men had jobs that used so much of their time that they could do little else. However, usually couples who were rated high on their acceptance of the role of spouse did actually spend a great deal of time together.

Where one spouse expressed dislike of the company of the other and avoided it, or complained a good deal about the activities that the partner enjoyed, he or she was rated very low in acceptance of the spouse role. Table 27 presents the cross-tabulations of the partners' acceptance of the role of spouse with the emotional health of the children. Scores of 5 indicate complete acceptance and scores of 0, no acceptance.

It can be seen that families in which the spouse role was well accepted by the husband and wife had almost equal numbers of healthy and disturbed children; hence acceptance of the spouse role seems to be no guarantee of emotional health. However, it should be noted that such families produced the largest proportion of emotionally healthy children found in the subsample. More important is the finding that families in which husband and wife rejected the spouse roles tended to produce emotionally disturbed children.

Table 27

PARENTS' ACCEPTANCE OF SPOUSE ROLES AND EMOTIONAL HEALTH OF CHILDREN

Emotional health of children	Role acceptance[a]											
	Husband			Wife			Together					
	H	I	L	H	I	L	5&5	5&3	5&1	3&3	3&1	1&1
Healthy	13	2	5	11	4	5	11	2	0	2	1	4
Intermediate	2	0	3	2	0	3	2	0	0	0	0	3
Disturbed	10	0	10	8	3	9	8	2	0	1	0	9

[a] H = High; I = Intermediate; L = Low.

These findings seem to reflect another observation made in the course of the study: that the relationship between the husband and wife is critical to the emotional health of the children. Though disturbed children are found in families in which husband and wife score high on degree of acceptance of their spouse roles and healthy children appear in families with low scores, it does seem that acceptance influences the emotional health of the children. We suspect that the reason that the correlation is not stronger is that role acceptance does not necessarily mean that the spouses play their roles well, nor that the relationshsip as set up is functional to the needs of the members of the family psychologically, socially, and culturally.

In the pilot study, as in the larger study reported above, we found a positive relationship between the degree to which husband and wife accepted their roles as spouses and the emotional health of the children. We became interested in how their acceptance of their roles had come about, and after an intensive investigation of their relationships, arrived at two interesting insights. In the first place, we noted that there seemed to be an association (we must say "seemed" because the sample in the pilot study consisted of only nine couples) between the strength of the father's role and the warmth of the husband-wife relationship. The optimal relationship seemed to develop when there was a father-led, but not a father-dominant, authority structure in the family. (See Chapter Six.) This appears to be a structure of authority gratifying to both the husband and wife, probably because it reinforces their sexual identities and provides a smooth basis for interaction.

We noted that wives who most completely accepted their spouse and housewife roles had an attitude toward their husbands that was so admiring that we labeled it the "adoration pattern." The following statements typify this attitude:

I thought he was wonderful, and I feel even more so today. I realize that I wouldn't be able to get along without him. He is so nice. I always tell my daughter that if she is ever lucky enough to get a man who is as grand as her father is to me, I'll think she struck oil. I felt that my guardian angel was really looking after me. We still feel that way.

My marriage has been good for me. It brought out an awful lot of good things in me I never knew I had. My husband made life for me. I guess I was starved for love before I met him, and he has fulfilled a great need in me for that.

My marriage has been just as good as it could possibly be. I feel so grateful that it's been so good in every respect. I've been more than lucky.

He is one of the nicest men I have ever known—kind, considerate, thoughtful, hardworking, and conscientious. He is a wonderful father and a wonderful husband. He is very patient and kind and very good.

We felt that all this was most unusual and wondered how it had come about. When we looked into family backgrounds of the adoring wives we discovered that all had suffered from intense maternal deprivation. In every case they said that their mothers had been domineering, manipulative, and cold, and their fathers soft, loving, and nonmanipulative. Actually, some of the fathers had been inadequate as males—occupational failures or alcoholics —but in contrast to the rejecting mothers they had seemed to be positive. Some of the reports may have been heavily laden with fantasy, but this does not alter the image: the wives had felt deprived in mothering and found compensation in fathering. Of course, there is a distinct possibility that these memories or feelings were defensive screens that they used to sever their infantile attachment to their mothers and to account for their erotic attachment to their fathers, but our data did not permit us to test this hypothesis. However, whatever the reasons, it does seem clear that they had developed dependency on their fathers for emotional support. When they married the pattern of dependency was evidently transferred to their husbands. If the husband was strong and supportive, kind and loving, the basic attitude of the wife grew stronger and developed into the adoration pattern. All the husbands in the pilot study were kind and supportive, but only four of them were also strong. In these four cases the wives enjoyed a strong sense of security and fulfillment, which they expressed in the adoration pattern.

In the other five cases, where strength in the husbands was absent or minimal, a different mechanism seemed to operate. Here the wife often seemed to be the strong member of the pair, offering her husband varying degrees of support. In contrast to the four strong husbands, these five husbands were primarily passive. Their wives gave them love, strength, and support in exchange for kindness, softness, and devotion.

In the larger study, though we did find the adoration pattern underlying many good marriage relationships, and never found it associated with poor relationships, we discovered that it was by no means the sole basis of a good marriage or a high degree of role acceptance. In fact we have come to the conclusion that it is not the best basis; the best basis, we found, was a high level of emotional health and maturity in the wife instead of an unresolved infantile dependency.

RECIPROCITY OF SOCIAL ROLES

Social roles, as patterned activities and interactions that are part of a social system, are naturally interdependent. In the family, the role of father is a pattern of activities, duties, and rights related to the roles of children. The father role is defined by the community, but the father can only play that role if the children accept it. If they fail to play their reciprocal roles, or play them inadequately or in a distorted way, it will be hard for him to play his role. If they reject their roles, as in fact they are likely to do as they grow older, he can no longer play his, though he may keep on trying.

Ordinarily, within a particular social system a person has a set of roles—for example, head of the family, spouse, and father— which should be mutually supportive. As we have pointed out, success in one area often implies success in another. Of course, the ultimate standards of success must be those of the participants and not of the observer. People may sometimes invest most of their energies in a single role to the detriment of the others, or they may be able to play only one successfully. Thus the fact that the roles played by one person within a social system are interrelated does not mean that success in one insures success in the others; it simply means that the quality of performance in one affects performance in the others.

The reciprocicty of roles played by different members of the system is yet another matter, but can be thought of similarly, since here the quality of the role performance of one person affects that of others. As a case in point, let us consider the roles of husband and wife. These roles require certain reciprocal obligations, among which are care and companionship. The husband is expected to offer his wife care, affection, and respect, and the wife is expected to reciprocate. When each plays his part, a process of interaction is set in motion that is mutually supportive and facilitating. When the husband supports and cherishes his wife and is strong and assertive, she can securely and smoothly respond and yield; she will feel loved and protected and want to care for him. There are rules to this game, which if followed by both players permit the game to go on, but which, if neglected by one, leave the other bewildered, unable to act, and perhaps angry. These rules always include a concern with the dignity and self-respect of the other because the self is always bound up in the game. Thus the husband who fails to be strong and assertive is bound to have a wife who feels incomplete because she is thwarted in playing her role of woman according to the rules of her society. Though this is a rich and complicated area, here we simply draw attention to the general idea that roles are interdependent; when one of the actors rejects his role or plays it incompletely, the drama is disrupted.

Since compatibility between the roles of a single player in a particular social system is necessary, it seems likely that if one role relationship is interrupted, the player may be subjected to strains, causing him to do badly in his other roles. The classic example is of the parent who, playing his spouse role inadequately, misplays his parent role and rejects or seduces his child. The etiology of these misplays can, of course, be traced back to the family of orientation. If, as a child, the individual experiences an inadequate child-parent relationship, he may seek to redress it in the relationship with his marriage partner, thus misplaying his spouse role, and by rendering that relationship inadequate, misplay his parent role as well.

Role interaction is important because it is linked with the self-concepts and emotions of the players. Ordinarily, the culture and the society lay down the criteria of personal adequacy connected with performance of a role. An individual judges his adequacy by how well he lives up to the social definitions of him as man, father, lawyer, lover, and so on. The most important roles are the ones that involve him with those emotionally important to him, and vice versa. A gratifying relationship is one in which he feels that he is playing his role competently and that others recognize, appreciate, and facilitate his performance. To a considerable extent it is these role experiences, and particularly the responses of the audience of emotionally important people, that give him a sense of worth and adequacy or worthlessness and inadequacy.

Our data indicated quite clearly that the emotional health of the children is strongly affected by the mother's adequacy in her mother role. This we believe to be one reason why the acceptance of spouse roles correlates with the emotional health of the children. We add that since it is probable that the children directly internalize the structure of the relationship between their parents, as a means of relating the parts of the self represented by the introjected mother and father figures, that relationship in itself immediately influences the emotional health of the children.

The findings presented in this chapter refer only to the husband's and wife's acceptance of their family roles. However, since these roles constitute the basic framework of the families' interactions, they both affect and reflect all parts of its functioning, and involve the personalities of its members. Roles, we suggest, must always be seen by the actors as manifestations of themselves, so that to some extent everyone measures himself by his success as a role player. If he likes his role, he probably likes himself and those who play the counter roles. If he rejects his role, he probably also rejects himself and dislikes the counter role players. The greater the emotional investment in the scene, and thus the roles, the greater the degree to which this will be true. Since the family is almost always of great emotional importance to its members, the roles they play should powerfully influence how they feel about themselves and each other, and thus in turn the functioning of the family and the emotional health of its members.

CHAPTER 9

Dimensions of Emotional Health

I t is our thesis that personality is, to an important extent, a reflection of the organization and relationships of the family in which it originates. We have dissected important dimensions of family life, showing how variations in each are related to emotional health or illness. Work, power, status, roles, and psychodynamics are the dimensions we chose. They do not do justice to the complexity and subtlety of family relationships, but they are the only ones we could measure, even crudely, and they are what this book has been about.

Chapter by chapter, we have tried to stick close to the can-

ons of scientific integrity, restricting ourselves to objectively determined facts and letting them speak for themselves. Now that the
job is done, we make a free-hand description and interpretation of
what we have found.

Our most important finding was that children's emotional
health is closely related to the emotional relationships between their
parents. When these relationships were warm and constructive, such
that the husband and wife felt loved, admired, and encouraged to
act in ways that they themselves admired, the children were happy
and healthy. Couples who were emotionally close, meeting each
other's needs and encouraging positive self-images in each other,
became good parents. Since they met each other's needs, they did
not use their children to live out their needs; since they were happy
and satisfied, they could support and meet their children's needs;
and since their own identities were clarified, they saw their children
as distinct from themselves. All this helped the children become
emotionally healthy people.

This positive relationship between husband and wife did not
depend on their being emotionally healthy themselves, though quite
clearly it was a great help. In some cases, the husband and wife
were emotionally disturbed, but still managed to set up a good
matrimonial relationship. When this happened, the children were
emotionally healthy; it seemed as if the good marital relationship
of the parents had insulated the children from the parents' emotional deficiencies.

Thus we found that the root of emotional health in children
was a good relationship between their parents. We discovered this
early, but were left with questions as to the basic ingredients and
etiology of such relationships. Seeking this information, we turned
to the time when these people found and selected each other in the
market place of matrimony, and thus to the rating and dating system of North America. In studying this process, we immediately
became conscious of that ubiquitous and powerful sociological
spirit: status.

People, it is said, marry for love. If this is the case, love is
a pious force yoked to propriety. People have a curious tendency
to fall in love with those who are socially suitable, probably because

the ways in which they meet and what they find attractive in each other depend on their backgrounds. The stress on romantic love, however, reveals that they are not conscious of the values that guide their choices. These values define good and bad marriages, and are to a considerable extent built into the dating process itself. The qualities that boys and girls seek in each other are predictive of those they will seek in marriage. Girls generally boast of the social skills and status characteristics of their dates—their dancing, their cars, and the places they went. Boys boast of the physical appearance, social skills, and cooperativeness of the girls. Later, when they marry, girls are said to make a good marriage when they marry a successful or up-and-coming man, boys when they marry a beautiful, charming, and faithful girl. To some degree then, the attributes of a successful marriage (from the girl's viewpoint) can be translated into social status. A marriage is successful when a girl marries a man of higher social status than herself. Since social status was a dimension we could pin down, and even measure, we used it as a starting point for our analysis. It proved to have an enormous payoff.

Briefly, we found that women who married up tended to be emotionally healthy, to marry emotionally healthy men, to have satisfying emotional and sexual relationships with their husbands, and to have emotionally healthy sons. For women who married down, the opposite was true. Presumably, the emotionally healthy girl was in tune with her culture and felt strong and attractive enough to try for a high-status, emotionally healthy man. When she succeeded, she was confirmed in her worth both by the approval of the community and the continued high status she enjoyed, and she was supported by the very positive relationship she found with her husband. Finally, since her children tended to be emotionally healthy, they too were rewarding.

The matter deserves close inspection, for it reaches into the personalities of the husband and wife and into their relationship in many ways. Status is the counterimage of self-esteem. In a highly mobile society like ours, where men are soon uprooted from their clans and communities, social status, particularly occupational status, becomes the real badge of identity and measure of self-esteem.

The woman who marries a successful man shares in his feeling of success. And the woman who marries a man of higher status than herself in a sense receives from him this status, and thereby permits him to give her this status; he thus seems strong and masculine and caring for her—both to her and to himself. This makes for a good heterosexual relationship.

Where the reverse is true, the woman feels degraded and blames the man who has done it to her. Furthermore, she is hardly in a receptive posture, and he has nothing to give, all of which makes for a strained and angry marital relationship. Small wonder that they are unhappy, that they tend to give up sex, and finally, that their children are often emotionally disturbed.

What is amazing is that status can make such a difference within the privacy of the family. Evidently, however, it lies close to our humanity, to the essentially social nature of self, and to our conception of life. We know that men find status important enough to die for. On second thought, then, perhaps its importance in the life of the family is not surprising.

On whatever basis the family is formed, it ordinarily results in a household, and with it, housework and a division of labor. In the world at large, a man's work is the key to his identity, to his power and rewards, and to his social fate. Within the family, it becomes part of the fabric of emotional relationships. We found that our families differed in the ways in which they divided up the work, and that these differences had meaning for the needs of the husband and wife and for the functioning of the family.

To begin with, the couple could choose how much work each was to do and how much they would share. Usually, each took responsibility for tasks appropriate to his sex: the man for the heavy work and finances, the woman for cooking and cleaning, and both for the care of the children. Yet how much they shared and what each took for his own varied from family to family, and the differences proved to be important. They were important because they shaped the relationship between the couple. We found that a balance of sharing and individual responsibility was most conducive to a mature and loving relationship between the husband and wife and to emotional health in their children. We reasoned that individual responsibility provided the basis for distinctive sex roles, as well as a means by which the husband and wife could demonstrate their love for each other by working in each other's interest. Shared activities gave something in common and thus created a bond between them. Couples who lacked either distinctive work roles or shared responsibilities had weaker relationships. Without sharing, relationships tended to be remote and formal. Without difference, they tended to be sibling-like.

The family with a balanced division of labor proved to be the only one in which the majority of couples had a vigorous sex life and experienced increasing satisfaction with their sexual relationship, had a good marital relationship, and had emotionally healthy children. Though it is true that this was also the only type of family in which the majority of husbands and wives were emotionally healthy, we still found that there was a direct relationship between the division of labor and the emotional health of the children. When we divided all the families into those with emotionally healthy parents and those with disturbed parents, we found that in each group those families with a balanced division of labor still had the largest proportion of emotionally healthy children. This is persuasive evidence of the powerful influence of the division of labor in the family.

Why is this influence so powerful? We think because it constitutes a fundamental pattern of relationships within the family, one that is directly observable and reiterated day in and day out throughout the lifetime of the family. For the members of the family, this is the way in which the world works, it is the way people relate, and it is the framework within which they must find and express themselves. Since, as we have suggested earlier, it carries great emotional import for the members of the family, its observability and repetition must have a great influence.

The balance of power in the family, though influenced to an extent by the couple's own psychological needs, generally conforms to the expectations of their culture. Most of the families in our study chose some kind of democratic pattern of shared decision making and responsibility. This is what is approved by the community, and it seems to be the most successful. Extreme dominance

by the husband or the wife is disapproved in our society and perhaps for that reason is incompatible with a successful marriage and
emotionally healthy children.

We identified four types of family: father-dominant, father-led, equalitarian, and mother-dominant. Both father-led and
equalitarian families are democratic, but in the equalitarian family
all decisions are shared, and husband and wife considered equal in
authority, whereas in the father-led family, though decisions are
arrived at through discussion, the husband is considered the boss
and has the final word.

The father-led type had the largest proportion of emotionally healthy children, followed by the father-dominant, the equalitarian, and the mother-dominant, in that order. In agreement with
most other studies, we found that the mother-dominant form was
extremely destructive of family authority and that almost none of
the children in these families were emotionally healthy. As far as
we could see, these were families with extremely unhappy mothers
and cold, impersonal family relationships.

A battery of personality tests administered to the children
revealed that these different types of family authority developed
different steps of personality in the children. The children from
father-dominant families were timid, withdrawn, submissive, and
without self-confidence, but also compulsive, self-disciplined, and
industrious. The children from mother-dominant families were just
as timid and withdrawn, but they lacked self-discipline and industry and showed serious psychopathologic symptoms. In contrast,
both equalitarian and father-led families were better off. The children from equalitarian families were quiet, friendly, industrious,
probably good followers and members; those from father-led families were more assertive and stable, probably good leaders.

Family relationships develop within a framework of roles;
that is, they are guided by cultural expectations as to the conduct
of husbands, fathers, children, wives, and mothers. We pulled the
husband's and wife's roles apart into their components of work,
spouse, and parent roles and found that the ways in which husband
and wife played their spouse and parent roles were closely related
to the functioning of the family and the emotional health of the

children. In each case, we were interested both in the extent to which the husband and wife accepted their roles and in the extent to which they practiced their roles.

We found that where both parents fully accepted their spouse roles, more than half of the children were emotionally healthy, and where both rejected these roles, more than half were emotionally disturbed. We used reported frequency of sexual intercourse and increasing or declining satisfaction with sex relations as indicators of the degree to which the parents were active in their spouse roles. We found that activity was strongly related to emotional health in the children (seventeen out of the twenty-six children of active parents were healthy), but that inactivity was not predictive of emotional disturbance in children. We concluded that high frequency and satisfaction with sexual relationships were good indicators of warm and loving family relationships and thus related to emotional health, but that low frequency and reported dissatisfaction were not good indicators of bad husband-wife relationships. This was confirmed by case studies in which we found some couples with excellent relations and emotionally healthy children, but with almost no sex life. This was a surprise, and though we believe such couples to be an exception, we cannot prove it.

The role of parent proved to be both more predictive of the emotional health of children and more dramatic in providing insights into the process by which parental care is translated into children's emotional health. The full acceptance of the parent roles by both parents seems to be an insurance of emotional health in the children, for of the seven children of parents who accepted their parent roles, six were healthy and none were disturbed. The complete rejection of parent roles by both parents was actually predictive of emotional disturbance in the children; of the eleven children of rejecting couples, five were disturbed, and only one was healthy. In fact, we found that of the thirteen children of couples in which one of the parents completely rejected the parent role, nine children were emotionally disturbed and only one was healthy.

We examined how active these couples were in their parent roles by asking them to what extent each participated in a list of child-care tasks. We found that the father's care of daughters when they were babies and the mother's care of sons when they were children strongly influenced both the emotional health and personalities of the children. Specifically, the fathers' care of daughters when they were babies significantly correlated with the daughters' emotional health, sociability, ego strength, dominance-confidence, and dominance; while the mothers' care of sons as children was significantly correlated with the sons' emotional health, ascendance, hypomania, sociability, self-acceptance, and extroversion. It is apparent from these findings that child care by the parent of the opposite sex is critical to the development of a positive sexual identity by the child. Simply stated, the child needs acceptance as a male or female by the parent of the opposite sex if he or she is to grow up to be emotionally healthy. To gain this acceptance, the child must present itself sexually to the parent of the opposite sex, and this presentation must be neither accepted nor rejected. This poses an especially tense situation in a cultural setting such as ours, which is fraught with sexual tensions. In this situation, the father who has a solid care relationship to his daughter before she makes these advances can accept her without accepting or rejecting the advances, and the mother who is involved with her son's activities can permit her baby to be one of the men in her life without accepting or rejecting these advances. Since the acquisition of sexual identity is a critical stage in the development of the child's emotional health, we think this is an important discovery.

In this study, we could not really take on the problem of psychodynamics in its full depth. We had to restrict ourselves to looking into the emotional meaning that each member of the family had for the others, and to searching for patterns of family psychodynamics that might be related to emotional health and illness. Our data consisted of a series of psychiatric judgments about various aspects of family functioning, such as communication, problem solution, the handling of affect, and so on. Ultimately, we grouped all these various judgments into two broad categories: problem solution-communication and autonomy. Each proved to be closely related to emotional health and illness. However, the reader is cautioned that since both the individual judgments and the emotional health ratings were made by the same psychiatrist, there is a very strong chance of contamination. While this, quite clearly, raises questions about the validity of these findings, there is an important sense in which the findings should not be overlooked—that is, as descriptions of families that foster or impede the development of emotional health in children. It is our judgment that problem solution-communication and autonomy are important dimensions in the development of emotional health and illness. We recognize, however, that they need careful testing.

Problem solution refers to the capacity of the family to recognize and solve emotional problems. No family is without such problems, but some families meet them head on and work hard to solve them. Others avoid or do not even see the problems; thus while they may go away, they are never solved. The problem-solving family has few problems, but the non-problem-solving family is overwhelmed with them. Furthermore, the children from problem-solving families were overwhelmingly healthy (fourteen out of eighteen), while those from non-problem-solving families were usually disturbed (eighteen out of twenty-eight).

Our data indicate that, contrary to popular opinion, it is the father, not the mother, who is important in problem solution. We suppose that this is true because he is usually the member who is most detached from the emotional flux of everyday family life, for to see the emotional problems of others one must be detached from them oneself.

Autonomy refers to the capacity of the family to permit its members separate emotional lives. It can be contrasted with the tendency of the members to huddle, or to stick so close to the others that no individuality is possible. In autonomous families, the individuality of each family member is encouraged and enjoyed by the others. Autonomy bears upon the recurrent human problem of separation from the parents and achievement of adulthood. It is a difficult battle for every child to leave his parents' love and security and to step out into the world, declaring himself an adult. It is also difficult for the parents to relinquish the gratification of caring for their children. The solution of this problem is critical for the development of emotional health. Our data support this, for the children from high-autonomy families tended to be healthy (eighteen out of twenty-seven), while those from low-autonomy families were overwhelmingly emotionally disturbed (twelve out of sixteen).

The key person in the development of autonomy seems to be the mother. Again this is surprising, for it is ordinarily assumed that it is the father who pushes the dependent son to go out and earn his own living. In fact, it is just the opposite, for autonomy is a product of the day-to-day decisions of family life, and it is the mother who makes these decisions. How far will she let her child go? With whom may he play? When may he decide for himself? It is through decisions like these that autonomy is either encouraged or discouraged.

With this summary completed, we return to the major finding of our study—that the relationship between the parents is critical to the emotional development of the children. If his parents have a positive status relationship (the father being of higher status than the mother), a balanced division of labor, and a father-led pattern of authority, the child is almost certain to be emotionally healthy. We assume that this is because such a positive organization supports emotional health in the parents, insulates the child from their emotional disturbances, and provides an approach to problem solution that the child can internalize.

Analysis of Data

The analysis of the data was difficult. Though in many cases we had included known scales as part of our sociological questionnaire, we found that we had very little confidence in most of these, and thus decided to construct our own. Our first task was the identification and measurement of variables. These fell into two groups: the sociological variables, such as the division of labor, the pattern of authority, communications, kinship relations, friendship relations, activities, and the like, and the psychodynamic variables describing the emotional relationships among family members and the emotional climate of family life. In each case we formulated questions based on our experience in the pilot study and on other studies that had been done in this field. Thus, for example, the sociological questionnaire contained extensive lists of questions about the division of labor based on the

Herbst scale, and questions about family integration based on the Cavan scale, and our interview approaches to the handling and expression of affect in the family were based on ideas raised by the pilot study.

We began our analysis of the data by isolating as many pertinent variables as we could. We immediately discovered that this was much easier to do in the case of the sociological variables. In each case we tried to construct a crude scale on which the categories or scores were defined with sufficient clarity in terms of the operations performed to assure inter-rater reliability. Ordinarily, our only test of the validity of the scales was their reasonableness plus our knowledge of certain key families. Thus, for example, since our questions about family work just about exhaust that area, and since each question has only three possible answers, each of which has a specific score value, there is no problem in inter-rater reliability. On grounds of reasonableness it seems likely that the people whom the family rates as usually doing a particular job actually do it. And finally, we got to know some families so well that we knew who did what and were able to see whether the actual division of labor was reflected in the answers to the questionnaire. Thus in many cases we could validate our scales only through the case history data. In one case (Bruck, 1963) we had an independent study that validated our measure of authority in the family.

We found the task much more difficult in the case of the psychiatric variables, particularly those describing the relationships among family members and the general emotional climate of family life. In the first place, it is very difficult to devise operational definitions of these variables since the psychiatrist normally takes into consideration a kind of Gestalt when making his judgments. Secondly, since many of these variables necessarily dealt with feeling states rather than patterns of behavior, it was possible to interpret the same datum in different ways, depending on the people involved, and different data often indicated the same thing. We made one serious attempt to establish the reliability of the psychodynamic variables by having two independent assessments made by different psychiatrists, but the results were unsatisfactory. Though there was broad agreement on the general psychodynamic characteristics of each family, there was much less agreement on the exact degree to which the family was characterized by, for example, the expression of hostility. Thus except for the area of emotional health we were unable to quantify, even very crudely, the psychodynamic variables.

Our emotional health ratings were another matter. Their reliability was, in our opinion, established by the high level of agreement between the two raters, and by the fact that in all cross-tabulations we established a broad intermediate, or neutral, category consisting of the central part of the distribution. The validity of the ratings showed up in various parts of the study in terms of the differential behavior of the subjects: first, in the differential degree to which subjects of different degrees of emotional health cooperated in the study, and second, in classical areas like sexual behavior. Thus we are confident that within reasonable limits our emotional health ratings are both reliable and valid.

There was, of course, no difficulty with the psychological tests since they had already been scaled. However, in many cases we felt that since they were likely to be most valid in the extremes, or even in just one extreme, they were more useful when divided into three or four crude categories.

We used two measures of relationship: correlations and cross-tabulations with chi square. The first proved unproductive, but since it took an enormous amount of time and energy the attempt should be described.

Correlations provide one with a measure of the degree to which two variables are related, as well as an idea of the extent to which the relationship might have occurred by chance alone. Naturally, we sought this information. However, there was still another problem that led our analysis in the direction of correlations. This was our feeling that the various aspects of family life were interrelated in very complex ways. We felt that we might be able to understand these relationships better if we could intercorrelate all the relevant variables. Therefore we set up a computer program that would intercorrelate 110 variables, or all the major sociological and psychological variables that we had been able to measure. We ran this program three times, once for boys alone, once for girls alone, and once for the two together. As a result we had an enormous number of coefficients of correlation, since for each variable —for example, the degree to which the father participated in the care of the children—we had its correlation with each of the other 109 variables for boys alone, for girls alone, and for both together. At this point the analysis bogged down, for we became involved in very complex problems of interpretation.

In matrices like this, ordinary measures of probability are disturbed. For example, if one runs 100 correlations between the same variables with samples of the same size, according to the laws of probability one will get a certain number of correlations of each level of significance by chance alone. Thus if one runs 100 correlations, or, as in our case, thousands of correlations, how does one interpret even an ordinary statistically significant correlation? We chose the defense of patterns, so that if a group of variables was seen as linked in theory, and if the correlations showed the linkage, we assumed that they were in fact related. Following this idea, we identified many interesting patterns, among which was that of a broad difference in the importance of certain variables for the emotional health of boys and of girls. But only where we had a clearly defensible theoretical and common-sense basis for the correlations that appeared did we feel justified in using them. Actually, it should be possible to establish the probabilities of the appearance of certain groups of intercorrelations, but this was beyond our statistical sophistication, and in fact beyond what we felt would be justified by the thoroughness of our sampling procedures, or by the accuracy and reliability of our measuring devices. Thus, though we had committed an enormous amount of time to this aspect of the analysis, we used the results very sparingly and only where they were supported by theory and other findings.

Instead, we used the correlational matrix as an exploration device, and where we found strong and patterned correlations, we made a detailed case study and cross-tabulation of the variables in question. The cross-tabulation had, in our estimation, two advantages: the detection of curvilinear relationships between variables and the identification of associations that only occurred in an extreme of the distributions. Furthermore, the use of these cross-tabulations plus the chi square did not involve the more elaborate assumptions necessary to the use of product-moment coefficients of correlation.

For the purpose of these cross-tabulations we ordinarily divided the distribution according to some mathematical principle—for example, into fifths, thirds, or quarters—though occasionally this had to be altered for particular frequency distributions. When these sociological variables were cross-tabulated with emotional health, emotional health was ordinarily divided into three categories: healthy, intermediate, and disturbed, with the idea that the misclassifications were likely to fall into the intermediate category. We then used McBee Keysort cards, setting up one card for each family in the sample and recording on the card both the actual scores in each variable and the category into which the family fell. These cards could then be very rapidly hand-sorted to establish the cross-tabulation as well as the controls. When this was done, we had three kinds of findings about the relationship between variables: the correlations for boys, for girls, and for the entire group; the cross-tabulations; and the comparative case materials from the two groups of families in the extremes of healthy and disturbed.

The analytic process thus had a history. First there was the attempt to identify and to measure the key variables. At this stage some of the variables in which we had been interested were discarded, either because we found that we simply did not have a reasonable amount of reliable data or because we could not measure it. This was the case with communications in the family. In the second stage, the analysis of the relationship between variables, we used alternative modes of analysis: correlations, cross-tabulations, and the comparison of the extremes, and in this process still more of our variables were discarded because they appeared to have no influence or because we discovered that they were in fact only variants of other variables. For example, the division of labor had been subdivided into thirty-eight subareas, including, for example, the father's participation in housework, and the difference in the degree to which the father and the mother participated in the control of finances. Ultimately, we restricted our analysis to the division of labor variables that were most inclusive of participation in that area, such as the total participation of the father and the mother, in the work of the family.

In most cases we had parallel information from each member of the family and were thus in a position to compare their statements. Though there was always some variation, we found that the mother's ratings were usually those of the majority of the family, so we used her responses to describe the family, except in cases in which we only had the information from the original subject. Thus, in general, the variables reported on in this book are those for which we had substantiation in depth—that is, in terms of the three ways in which we measured relationship.

The psychodynamic variables, except for the judgments about emotional health, were less well substantiated. As we indicated earlier, we were not able to establish operational definitions or reliability in scoring for these variables. We were thus faced with a dilemma: Our inability to substantiate these variables raised questions about the scientific basis of our findings in this area; yet we felt that we had valuable information on a clinical level that constituted an important contribution to knowledge. We decided to keep the material, but to make no bones about its character. The original data consisted of the transcripts of the psychiatric interviews with the members of the ten families at either extreme of our emotional health continuum. Using these transcriptions, the psychiatric director (who had made the original interviews)' analyzed each family in terms of a series of categories of family functioning that had been developed during the pilot study and refined in a hospital setting. When these family analyses were completed, they were turned over to a sociological research assistant for coding and cross-tabulations. Since the coding and cross-tabulations suggested that many of the categories used were in fact identical, though bearing different names, we regrouped them into broader categories, which we felt did represent significant dimensions of the emotional climate of family life.

What then were the basic problems that we had to face in the analysis of our data? The first was accuracy. Were our respondents telling us the truth? The answer is that in large measure they tried to do so and did. We were usually able to check their responses because we had identical information from all the members of the family and could compare responses. Where this was not possible, we had to rely on the consistency of the responses with others given by the respondent and on our perceptions of his life situation.

The second problem was to devise a reliable and valid method of measuring the dimensions of family life in which we were interested. In this task we emphasized descriptions of actual behavior rather than attitudes, since we felt that reports of behavior were more easily confirmed and less subject to distortion. Thus we were more interested in what our respondents actually did in terms of club participation, entertainment, and so on, and the number of times they did these things, than in how they felt about them or what they said they were most interested in. This emphasis facilitated not only accuracy in the data but also reliability, since with this kind of data it is easier to devise operational definitions for magnitude categories. For example, one can say that a high participator is a person who belongs to three or more clubs that he attends twice a month, or in which he is an officer, and a low participator one who belongs to fewer than three organizations and is an officer in none, and can thus be certain of complete reliability in categorizing respondents.

The validity of these categories as a measure of social activity is more difficult to establish. To some extent one can establish validity in these behavioral areas by inspecting the frequency distribution. Where there is a clear break in the distribution, so that some individuals cluster at one end of the continuum and others at the other, one can be fairly certain of a true difference in the degree of participation. Similarly, one can divide the distribution into thirds and think primarily in terms of the extremes. This procedure involves the assumption that the use of these criteria necessarily leads to some error in identifying degrees of participation, but that those who fall into the extremes will in fact be different. We always used this device in conjunction with the inspection of case histories: If our scale identified an individual as a high participator, we turned to the life history material for confirmation. Finally, one must always rely on common sense and on one's own experience to establish validity. Though it is clearly a mistake to rely on these alone, they remain fundamental and important validation tools when the researcher is completely familiar with the society he is studying.

There remained the problem of interpreting measures of relationship between variables. The choice of measures was made in accordance with the rules of statistical usage, so that, for example, we did not use a coefficient of correlation unless we felt that our sample and data met the necessary conditions. But even where they did meet these conditions, we had to raise questions about the linearity of the relationship, or whether the relationship might not in fact be different at one extreme of the continuum, and about relevance. Was the relationship one that we might expect in terms of our developing theory, and if not, could it be explained in terms of modification in the theory? In other words, did it fit in? In this matter one has to be alert for serendipity—the unexpected finding that leads to major theoretical gains.

Underlying all of this was the frame of reference that directed the analysis and raised the questions that we tried to answer. Here we made the effort to employ perspective by incongruity, looking at our problem in impious ways and employing alien frames of reference. This approach is exemplified by Parsons' (1951) view of the family as a therapeutic system, which gave him new insights into the socialization process. We ourselves were not as successful in doing this as we had hoped, and relied to a great extent on quite familiar and tried categories of analysis. However, we made some gains by considering the family as a business, with requirements for efficiency and order; as a stage for playing out status aspects of the larger social system; and finally, as an organization that responds to, and succeeds in terms of, the familiar three levels of human experience: the psychodynamic, the social, and the cultural. This last perspective is reported at length in Chapter Two.

APPENDIX **B**

Six Case Studies

CASE 1
(MALE, FIRST-YEAR UNIVERSITY STUDENT)

Subject talked very easily and well and had a fine sense of humor. He demonstrated sensitivity to what was going on inside himself as well as to what was going on around him. He was interested in a broad variety of areas and became quite involved while discussing them. He discussed his first few months at the university with intelligence and objectivity. He had found these few months "rough and miserable up to now." The reason for this was that in high school he really had not had to work very hard to get above average marks, but "things are different now. They're cutting me down to size." He found that he had so much work that "it is cramping my style." He was finding it difficult to keep involved in a variety of extracurricular interests, such as music and intra-

175

mural athletics, and still keep on top of his academic load. He was managing to do it, but obviously had to work quite hard in the process.

Asked if he had emotional problems, he replied: "I'm a moody character at times; mostly school work puts me there. If I feel behind, I get awful panicky and feel put in a corner. I get touchy. The smallest things irk me no end." Investigation of this complaint revealed a moderate degree of unconscious feelings of inadequacy and consequent self-doubts. The anxiety generated by these feelings was handled by a tendency toward mild compulsivity and was expressed by his need to be "on top of things," or in control, all of the time. The anxiety was mild and relatively infrequent, but at the time of the interview was current because of the process of adaptation to the strains of university life.

He described both parents and their relationship to him and each other at length, with great sensitivity and apparent objectivity. He was obviously fond of both parents, yet was able to criticize them and express some negative feelings in relation to some of their behavior and attitudes.

His history was quite normal. He was in touch with all his feelings and had no difficulty in the appropriate expression of any and all affects.

He dated girls frequently, with obvious pleasure and satisfaction. He devoted a fair amount of time to the usual adolescent preoccupations concerning the approach to the opposite sex, talking at length about his "techniques" of dealing with girls. He displayed little, if any, guilt over his sexual desires. "There's no point in going out with a girl who doesn't like what I like or believe in these things [necking and petting]. We'd only be matching wits with each other then." Though he stated he would like to have intercourse, he was still too fearful to go through with it. "I suppose I'd like to have it, but I am too chicken to walk into a drug store and ask for condoms, and I can't see myself having intercourse without them."

His statements with reference to his life goals were very realistic, sensitive, rich, and well thought out, and his self-image was very perceptive, well constructed, and quite sensitive.

The psychological tests confirmed the interview findings for this subject. They indicated some mild anxiety with reference to sexuality and feelings of inadequacy. According to our criteria, this subject was given a rating of A-2. There were no structured psychiatric symptoms. He was very well adapted in both the social and occupational spheres. His dynamic integration was sound. The mild anxiety generated by his sexual fears and his slight feelings of inadequacy were well controlled and bound.

CASE 2
(FEMALE, FIRST-YEAR UNIVERSITY STUDENT)

Subject was intelligent, attractive, and somewhat more mature in appearance than most of the other freshman subjects. She did not display much anxiety during the interview and showed interest and involvement in the interview situation.

Subject had worked for a year following graduation from high school because she needed the money and because she was not clear about what she wanted to do. She was still undecided as to choice of career before marriage, though she had narrowed down the choices. She was enjoying the university very much, liked the subjects she was taking, and appreciated the opportunity to make new friends.

Asked whether she had any emotional problems, she stated: "I get scared when exams come along. I bite my fingernails and I get the feeling I won't be able to study all the work." She also reported getting mildly depressed at times for no apparent reason. This happened every few months, usually following some disappointment, and occurred particularly when she was alone in the house on a dark, dreary day. "I wander around the house feeling lost and that nobody cares. I go up to my room and do my homework and then it goes away. It doesn't last more than a day or so."

Subject was able to describe both parents, the interparental relationships and her relationship to them with objectivity and clarity. She was quite fond of both parents, especially her father. She got along better with her father than her mother "because I think mother and I have the same temperament." She got along well with her parents and siblings, though they had the usual arguments. She argued most with her mother, but usually her father would cut in after a while and tell her to stop, and "this will be it." Her arguments with her father were "usually sane arguments. We talk things out. No yelling back and forth."

Her background and developmental history were not remarkable. There was no evidence of neurotic conflicts or problems. She was in touch with most of her feelings and able to respond emotionally to appropriate stimuli. She felt that she had a quick temper that boiled up fairly easily, but did not have too much difficulty in curbing it when necessary. She made friends easily and well. She had a wide circle of acquaintances and several close friends with whom she felt very intimate.

She indicated some difficulty in the sexual sphere. She felt guilty over her sexual arousal while petting with her boy friends. She seemed to go out of her way to curb herself in this area, out of guilt. In fact she seemed to be attracted to her present boy friend largely because of his sexual passivity; to a certain extent she used him as a defense against her own guilty fear of her sexual impulses. She was going "steadily" with this boy rather than "steady." (This was a differentiation of degree utilized by these adolescents to indicate a lesser degree of commitment to the relationship. Going "steadily" means that either partner may feel free to date others.) She didn't want to go "steady" with a boy: "I don't want to feel too sure of him because then I'm afraid I can't care enough about him." Here she seemed to be indicating her fear of heterosexual intimacy and her need for distance, as well as fear of the danger of sexual arousal.

She was quite clear as to her goals in life. She wanted a career for a few years and then marriage and a family. Her self-image was fairly clear, though not very deep or sensitive. She displayed a lot of self-respect and valued herself as a female and as an individual in her own right.

This subject displayed no structured psychiatric symptoms. She was well adapted socially and occupationally. Her occasional mild depressions and her guilt over her sexual impulses indicated a mild impairment of dynamic integration with related mild anxiety. She was rated B-2.

CASE 3
(FEMALE, FIRST-YEAR UNIVERSITY STUDENT)

Subject was a pretty girl, but one who did not pay much attention to her appearance. She was shy, inhibited, and quite tense and anxious throughout the interview. She denied the existence of any emotional problems or conflicts.

She was unable to describe either of her parents as people other than in terms of their interest in her schoolwork and their pattern of pushing and encouraging her to do well academically. Her description of them follows: "I think they are excellent parents. They cooperate and have great interest in my schoolwork and try to urge me on to do my best . . . very willing to help me if I have problems in schoolwork . . . will take all Sunday to help me with math problems. When you find yourself a little depressed at the whole thing—discouraged—they'll push you and encourage you to keep going . . . that things will be better if you keep at it. They are very reasonable in the things they allow me to do . . . don't restrict me. If something is harmful, they tell me schoolwork comes first and if that's all right, you can have your fun——about all I can say——good people and very sympathetic towards others." When asked to describe the parents further as people, as individuals in their own right, she stated: "Don't understand what you mean. They are kind people, use great judgment in whatever they do, try to make my brother and me think logically too. I don't know if I have answered your questions or not." Did she ever have fights with her parents? "No, we have our disagreements, but you can't get along with anyone perfectly all the time. I usually come to understand why they say those things. I come to feel that parents usually are right."

This girl seemed capable of structuring the world only in intellectual terms. She seemed totally out of touch with her feelings and went to great lengths to repress or deny them. What came across was a marked affective barrenness, almost like that in cases of severe emotional deprivation. She talked about how her parents "think logically" and how she tried to "think logically." It seemed obvious that she equated thinking logically with functioning with a total absence of affect.

She could not handle the expression of anger and had to deny and repress her rage at all times. At times she turned her rage in on herself, and she described crying occasionally in response to feeling hurt. She also tended to project her rage and felt vaguely that people were out to hurt her. Her feelings in this area were vague and bordered on the paranoid. "Some people can be hard and mean—not what they say, just their actions—and when you fight back sometimes they don't like it. They don't expect it." She made several statements of this sort. It was never very clear about what or whom she was talking. When she was pressed about this, she vaguely referred to a friend, but one had the feeling that she was probably talking about her family. Her frequent nightmares were an indication of her difficulties with rage. "Sometimes I dream about war, usually after reading a newspaper or history. I seem to be surrounded by soldiers and guns and everyone is firing at me and you don't seem to have a chance."

Her description of her past history was so barren that it was noncontributory.

She led a constricted and inhibited life with very few friends or acquaintances, most of her time being devoted to academic work. "I don't make friends easily. I'm usually backward and shy." She did not confide in friends or her parents. "I don't feel I should burden others—not that I have very many burdens."

She had no relationship with boys, having had only one date in her life. "I am pretty young to go out too much. I see downfalls in it. Some kids go steady and it breaks up and they are usually lost. They have lost the art of making friends and it's difficult for them." She denied any sexual fantasies or self-stimulation.

She had had a long-time interest in becoming a research chemist. Her life goals were wrapped up in this to the exclusion of all else. Her self-image and ego-identity were extremely hazy and confused, and she was unable to give any description of self.

This subject showed no structured psychiatric symptoms. She functioned in the occupational sphere in that she seemed to be doing well academically. However, she was very maladapted socially. She showed moderate to severe impairment of her dynamic integration, moderately severe psychopathology, and moderate amounts of anxiety. She repressed all affect and was affectively barren and flat. She had marked problems with rage and sexuality. Her ego-identity was shallow, hazy, and confused, and her life goals narrow and constricted. She was rated C-3.

CASE 4
(MALE, FIRST-YEAR UNIVERSITY STUDENT)

Subject was a handsome, clean-cut, well-dressed adolescent, looking younger than his stated age. He was sincere and eager to cooperate in the interview. He talked easily and well, except when discussing anxiety-laden areas, at which time he demonstrated marked blocking and difficulty. He liked university life, but was finding the courses most difficult. When asked about emotional problems, he said: "I get nervous over anything—talking to girls over the phone, exams, just about anything—so much so that I have an asthmatic condition and I am under medical treatment for it."

The condition from which he suffered was an asthmatic wheezing, which was triggered by anxiety-provoking situations. The symptom had first developed several years previously when he was faced with a situation that was particularly disturbing to him. It recurred every one to two months and lasted about a day each time. This subject had been troubled with severe anxiety throughout his life. Anxiety symptoms had always made schoolwork difficult for him, and his academic achievement had suffered accordingly. Despite medical advice, the family had never obtained psychiatric treatment for him.

He gave a very meager, constricted, nonperceptive picture of his parents and demonstrated little feeling in relation to them as people. "They are very nice——I get along with them fine——we have our squabbles now and then——but I wouldn't change them ——that's about all." When asked if that was all he could say about them, he replied: "I don't know what I can say——except Dad is hard-working and is pretty good with his hands. Mother is a good cook. I don't know what I could say——I'm stuck——."

He displayed marked jealousy and rage toward his older sister. "I just think she's spoiled. She has always gotten privileges that I never get."

Apart from difficulty in controlling his rage, which was primarily focused on his sister, he seemed incapable of experiencing any feelings other than his all-consuming anxiety. He showed this lack of feeling and marked constriction in every area of his life. It was obvious that his severe anxiety precluded any meaningful growth and development.

He experienced so much anxiety about sexuality that he blocked to the point of being unable to discuss it at all.

When asked to give a description of self, he was unable to do more than mumble a few confused statements referring to his problems with his anxiety. He was unable to think or talk about life goals in any coherent, meaningful manner.

The psychological tests confirmed the above picture and added more information about specific conflict areas. The following is an excerpt from the psychological evaluation: "The most striking features about this subject are his infantile dependency, marked sense of inadequacy and all-pervasive anxiety. There is serious confusion in sexual identification related to his passive dependent needs. The subject's ego structure is extremely immature and he is prevented by his reliance on massive repression from having any real awareness of his own feelings other than his generalized free-floating anxiety. There are no indications of any kind of mature interpersonal relationships. Though he has a strong desire for social contact and approval, it seems to be almost entirely related to his dependent, receptive needs. He feels quite isolated from his peers and tends to think of himself as a little child."

In this case there were present structured psychiatric symptoms, social and occupational maladaptation, severe psychopathology, and severe anxiety. There was no evidence of disturbed reality testing. He was rated D-1.

CASE 5 (MALE EXECUTIVE)

Subject was friendly, cooperative, intelligent, and sincere. He displayed mild to moderate tension throughout the interview.

He had no conscious awareness of any emotional symptoms or conflicts.

He described both parents adequately and with a lot of affection. They had both been dead for some years. He had been very close to his father, whom he described as a warm, soft, understanding man. They had spent a lot of time and done a lot of things together. He had not been as close to his mother, who had had a strong temper and who obviously had been the dominant one of the parents. He felt he resembled his father. He had felt considerable sorrow and grief on the death of his father. "It was not exactly unexpected. I think I knew it was coming. I felt a great void at the time. I shed a tear or two after the funeral. I would not say it was a shock, but I just felt something had gone out of my life that could not be replaced. There was a great difference in our ages, but I could always go to him for advice with troubles. He always had a sympathetic ear and good advice." His sorrow on the death of his mother had been definite and obvious but much less intense.

He had had a normal and healthy development and growth with no history of any neurotic problems. He had got along well with his siblings, related well to others, and done well at school. He had been very active in athletics and other hobbies and pastimes in his youth and still maintained some of these interests.

He had dated a number of girls and had an active social life in his youth. His sexual activities prior to marriage had been limited to necking and petting. "It was not a case of not wanting to do it [sexual intercourse] but of being afraid to do it."

He had been very successful in his business career. He worked hard at his job and was highly respected in his field. He also managed to lead an active family and social life. He discussed his children with warmth, interest, and perceptiveness. It was obvious that he enjoyed them and related well to them. He was able to give an objective and broad description of himself. He obviously derived great satisfaction, pride, and respect from his work and his place in the community.

He had never had much of a temper, but there were indications that he had difficulty in expressing rage and asserting himself in general. "I think I have a temperament like father—not to rise up, but to try and take the other person's point of view and to try and reason it out. My wife criticizes me today for that—that I am inclined to take the other person's point of view more than myself. I think she is right."

He was in touch with his feelings generally, despite his mild difficulties in expressing rage and asserting himself. He had a tendency to keep these feelings to himself. "I am not exactly outspoken. I get accused at times at home that you have to be a mind reader to know what I am thinking. My wife would tell you that you have to drag it out of me. She would be right."

There had been some difficulties in the marital sexual relationship. In the first few years following marriage, subject experienced premature ejaculation. For the last few years he had no longer had those difficulties, but there had been a diminution in frequency of intercourse, which now occurred on an average of once every two weeks. He found it difficult to discuss the sexual problems with his wife, though it was obvious that she was more than willing to do so. He felt that their sexual relations had improved in terms of mutual satisfaction over the years, even though he implied that his wife would like them to be more frequent.

This man had mild problems in the area of assertiveness and the expression of rage. He also had difficulties in his sexual functioning, which seemed to be related to some confusion and difficulty in sexual identification. This difficulty in sexual identification was related to unconscious conflict over his warm relationship with a soft, giving, and loving father and the hostility present in his relationship to an aggressive, dominant mother. This man's ego strength had been such that despite the presence of these unconscious sexual conflicts over the years he had been able to improve his sexual functioning to its present level, at which he experienced only a minimum amount of associated anxiety.

In this case there was an absence of structured psychiatric symptoms. The man was well adapted socially and occupationally, but there was mild to moderate impairment of dynamic integration with mild anxiety. He was rated B-3.

CASE 6 (FEMALE, HOUSEWIFE)

Subject was very tense and anxious throughout the interview. She projected an air of forced gaiety and friendliness, as if to cover the marked anxiety. She related to the interviewer in the somewhat bizarre manner of a woman fairly well along in middle age who tries to act like a teenager, using teen-age expressions quite frequently. She spoke in a disconnected, rambling, and illogical manner, so that it became very difficult to follow what she was saying and remain in touch. She had an eye-blinking tic, which, though barely perceptible at the beginning of the interview, became progressively more severe as the interview continued and her anxiety increased.

When asked whether she had any emotional conflicts or symptoms she replied "The dark, the dark. That's the only thing. Brother, I sure don't like the dark. I really think that's about all." She then went off on a rambling flight of words, the point of which seemed to be an attempt to describe an incident that had flared up her phobia of the dark.

This woman was unable to describe anyone or anything in a coherent, integrated fashion. Her description of her parents and her relationship to them had to be pieced together by the interviewer from a number of unrelated contexts. At one point she began to talk about the death of her mother, a number of years previously. When asked what her reaction had been to the death of her mother, she replied: "Well, I am the eldest. I have often had to take 'do this, do that,' as far as the eldest being concerned, yet I did not break down, yet I am not that cold. I come up and I don't break down, yet you won't even tell me." The interviewer then asked "Tell you what?" She replied: "The 'Why I do such and such a thing.'" She continued at great length implying she was angry with the interviewer for not giving her any psychiatric interpretations.

The picture she gave of her mother was that of a cold, self-centered, infantile, disturbed, domineering woman who was unable to give of herself to anyone. "I got along much better with her as she got older. This is a cruel thing to say, but she was more affectionate and understanding. As youngsters she was most undemonstrative——she was very possessive—she never gave us any credit for what we did. She never praised us. That's why we were so resentful——I always had to do things, and I'd say I didn't want to, but I had to do it or else. I was resentful, but I didn't do it graciously or willingly." These are verbatim statements referring to her mother, which were gathered from many different places in the interview. This woman was never able to defy or rebel against her mother, even though she described feeling angry and resentful. She had always had marked difficulty in coping with her rage and was obviously full of guilty fear as a result of the rage she had harbored all her life.

Asked if she had had a temper as a child, she replied, "No, strange thing is that they always said I was a yes-kid. I would agree with everybody——I think I was all very much inside. I'd do it, but I was feeling all the things inside me. You know. Oh, brother." Did she have a temper now? "I think I blow off now. I am not such a yes-person now. I can stand on my own two feet now. Yet I still get pushed around a lot. When people say something to me I take it. Then I say to myself, why didn't I talk back?"

How did she deal with her husband in arguments, when she was angry? "I do my best——but I don't make out so hot sometimes——many times I just shut up—— It takes too much out of me. But there is one thing—apparently I forget easily. I forget what I was so mad about and that makes me mad all over again. Why can't I remember what I was mad about?" This woman was so consumed by anxiety and guilty fears over her repressed rage that she appeared not to be in touch with any other feelings.

She described her father as a soft, affectionate man who was completely dominated and controlled by her mother. She remembered having a good relationship with him.

Her past history revealed she had had severe problems with her eye-blinking tic in grade school, where it had caused her much embarrassment. She had been very active and skilled in athletics and tended to be quite a tomboy. She had done well at school and seemed to get along with her peers. Her difficulties with her disturbed mother had made life unpleasant and unhappy at times.

She described the attitude toward sex in her home as being extremely puritanical and moralistic. She had been taught nothing about sexuality and had been made to feel extremely guilty about anything connected with it. She had been terrified and shocked by the onset of her menarche, not knowing what it was all about. "I came home from riding a bike and I thought I had hurt myself. Mother was in the era that everything was shush about sex, about pregnancy and women——oh so. It was terrible. That makes me mad. It was so wrong. Even in my second grade of high school I thought a baby came from the side. Boy, was I stupid. Not stupid —it was just ingrained in me. Yet now it's no different. Maybe they have gone to the other extreme in many instances."

She had had marked difficulties with her sexual adjustment throughout her married life. She had found the sex act very difficult for her and felt that it was wrong, bad, and disgusting. She had tried to avoid it as much as possible and the sexual relationship was now practically nonexistent in her marriage.

There was one child who had considerable difficulty in relating to her. She did not seem to have any understanding of this child and certainly was unable to give any meaningful picture of her as a human being. It would seem that this woman was so consumed with anxiety and conflict that she was unable to register much of what was going on about her.

Her description of herself was equally hazy, shallow, confused, and dominated by her anxiety and conflicts. When asked to describe herself, she replied: "I wish I were an even-keel type of person. I think it would be lovely to be a nice placid person. Oh gee. I am pooped out from being so excitable and running so. There are a lot of things I wish. I think we always want to be other than we are. That's right, isn't it? Women anyway. I suppose you men, you never bother about that."

This woman demonstrated the presence of structured psychiatric symptoms in the form of her tic and phobia. She was severely maladapted in both the social and occupational areas. She had marked difficulty relating to others and severe problems in being a wife and mother. Her psychopathology and anxiety were severe. She was so consumed with anxiety and guilty fear that her speech often became mere incoherent rambling. Her cognitive processes were obviously severely distorted as a result of her anxiety. She was markedly infantile, with severe conflicts over her unfulfilled dependency needs. She had severe problems in coping with her rage and aggression, a good deal of which she turned against herself. Her image of self was very devalued, and she demonstrated little, if any, self-esteem. She had marked feelings of inadequacy. Her sexual identification was exceedingly confused and distorted, with marked rejection of her femininity. She felt severe guilt over her sexuality and tended to reject her sexual impulses completely. Despite her tendency toward incoherence, there was no evidence of loss of contact with reality testing in the psychotic sense, although it was obvious that her ego functions were distorted and severely constricted. She was rated D-1.

References

ACKERMAN, N. W. *Psychodynamics of Family Life*. New York: Basic Books, 1958.

BLOOD, R. O., and WOLFE, D. M. *Husbands and Wives*. Glencoe, Ill.: Free Press, 1960.

BOTT, E. *Family and Social Networks*. London: Tavistock, 1957.

BRONFENBRENNER, U. "Some Familial Antecedents of Responsibility and Leadership in Adolescents." In L. Petrullo and B. Bass (Eds.), *Leadership and Interpersonal Behavior*. New York: Holt, 1961.

BRUCK, A. "Autocracy or Democracy: The Impact of Authority on the Family." Unpublished M.A. thesis, McGill University, 1963.

BURGESS, E. W., and LOCKE, H. J. *The Family*. New York: American Book, 1945.

CLAUSEN, J. A., and KOHN, M. L. "Social Relations and Schizophrenia: A Research Report and Perspective." In D. Jackson (Ed.), *The Etiology of Schizophrenia*. New York: Basic Books, 1960.

CRAWFORD, M. P. "Decision-making in Working Class English and Canadian Families." Unpublished M.A. thesis, McGill University, 1962.

DAWSON, A. Personal communication, 1952.

ERIKSON, E. H. "Growth and Crises of the Healthy Personality." In M. J. E. Senn (Ed.), *Symposium on the Healthy Personality*. Transactions of the Special Meetings of the Conference on Infancy and Childhood. New York: Josiah Macy, Jr. Foundation, June–July, 1950.

ERIKSON, E. H. "Identity and the Life Cycle." *Psychological Issues,* 1959, *1*(1).

Expert Committee on Mental Health of the World Health Organization, *Technical Report Series 31*. Geneva: April, 1951.

FROMM, E. *Escape from Freedom*. New York: Farrar, 1941.

GOODE, W. J. "Family and Mobility." Report submitted to the Institute of Life Insurance, no date.

HARTMANN, H. "Psychoanalysis and the Concept of Health." *International Journal of Psychoanalysis,* 1939, *20,* 308–321.

HERBST, P. G. "The Measurement of Family Relationships." *Human Relations,* 1952, *5,* 3–35.

HERBST, P. G. "Conceptual Framework for Studying the Family." In O. E. Oeser and S. B. Hammond (Eds.), *Social Structure and Family in a City*. London: Routledge and Kegan Paul, 1954.

HOLLINGSHEAD, A., and REDLICH, F. *Social Class and Mental Illness*. New York: Wiley, 1958.

HOMANS, G. *The Human Group*. New York: Harcourt, 1950.

HUGHES, E. C. *Men and Their Work*. Glencoe, Ill.: Free Press, 1958.

JACKSON, J. "Family Interaction, Family Homeostasis, and Some Implications for Congruent Family Therapy." In J. Masserman (Ed.), *Individual and Family Dynamics*. New York: Grune and Stratton, 1959.

JAHODA, M. "Toward a Social Psychology of Mental Health." In A. M. Rose (Ed.), *Mental Health and Mental Disorder*. New York: Norton, 1955.

JAHODA, M. *Current Concepts of Positive Mental Health*. New York: Basic Books, 1958.

KING, S. H., and HENRY, A. F. "Aggression and Cardiovascular Reactions Related to Parental Control over Behavior." *Journal of Abnormal and Social Psychology,* 1955, *50,* 206–214.

KINSEY, A. C., POMEROY, W. B., MARTIN, C. E., and GEBHARD, P. H. *Sexual Behavior in the Human Female*. Philadelphia: Saunders, 1953.

KOMAROVSKY, M. *The Unemployed Man and His Family*. New York: Dryden, 1940.

KOOS, E. L. *Families in Trouble*. New York: King's Crown Press, 1946.

KUBIE, L. "The Fundamental Nature of the Distinction Between Normality and Neurosis." *Psychoanalytic Quarterly,* 1954, *23,* 167–204.

LEIGHTON, D., HARDING, J. S., MACKLIN, V. D., MACMILLAN, A. M., and LEIGHTON, A. H. *The Character of Danger*. New York: Basic Books, 1963.

LEVY, M. J. *The Family Revolution in Modern China.* Cambridge: Harvard University Press, 1949.

LIDZ, T., and CORNELISON, A. R. "The Role of the Father in the Family." *American Journal of Psychiatry,* 1956, *5,* 113–126.

MACE, D. R. "The Employed Mother in the USSR." *Marriage and Family Living,* 1963, *23,* 330–334.

MASLOW, A. H. *Motivation and Personality.* New York: Harper, 1954.

MEAD, G. H. *Mind, Self, and Society.* Chicago: University of Chicago Press, 1934.

MENNINGER, K. *The Human Mind.* New York: Knopf, 1946.

MILLER, D. R., and SWANSON, C. *The Changing American Parent.* New York: Wiley, 1958.

PARSONS, T. *The Social System.* Glencoe, Ill.: Free Press, 1951.

RADO, S. "Theory and Therapy: The Theory of Schizotypal Organization and Its Application to the Treatment of Decompensated Schizotypal Behavior." In *The Psychoanalysis of Behavior,* Collected Papers Vol. II. New York: Grune and Stratton, 1962.

RADO, S. "Towards the Construction of an Organized Foundation for Clinical Psychiatry." *Comprehensive Psychiatry,* 1961, *2*(2), 65–73.

RIESMAN, D., GLAZER, N., and DENNY, R. *The Lonely Crowd.* Garden City, N.Y.: Doubleday, 1956.

RIEZLER, K. *Man: Mutable and Immutable.* Chicago: Regnery, 1950.

SCOTT, C. H. "Pattern of Child Adjustment." In O. E. Oeser and S. B. Hammond (Eds.), *Social Structure and Family in a City.* London: Routledge, 1954.

SROLE, L., LANGNER, T. S., MICHAEL, S. T., OPLER, M. K., and RENNIE, T. A. C. *Mental Health in the Metropolis.* New York: McGraw-Hill, 1962.

STRODTBECK, F. "Family Interaction, Values, and Achievements." In A. L. Baldwin, U. Bronfenbrenner, D. C. McClelland, and F. Strodtbeck, *Talent and Society.* Princeton, N.J.: Van Nostrand, 1958.

THOMAS, W. I. *The Unadjusted Girl.* London: Routledge, 1924.

WARNER, W. L., and ABEGGLEN, J. C. *Big Business Leaders in America.* New York: Harper, 1955.

WINCH, R. F. "The Theory of Complementary Needs in Mate Selection." *American Sociological Review,* 1955, *20,* 552–554.

WYNNE, L. C., IRVING, M. R., DAY, J., and HIRSCH, S. I. "Pseudomutuality in the Family Relations of Schizophrenics." *Psychiatry,* 1958, *21,* 205–220.

ZELDITCH, M. "Family, Marriage, and Kinship." In R. E. Favis (Ed.), *Handbook of Sociology.* Chicago: Rand McNally, 1964.

Index